D0841021

BULLETPROOF

By:

Laurie Beth Morales

Published by Motivational Press, Inc.
1777 Aurora Road
Melbourne, Florida, 32935
www.MotivationalPress.com

Manufactured in the United States of America.

ISBN: 978-1-62865-431-8

CONTENTS

PART THREE: A NEW DREAM

PART FOUR: REFLECTIONS

*"Out of suffering have
emerged the strongest souls.
The massive characters are
seared with scars."*

Khalil Gibran

It's OK Mom…

Alec and Asher, who have claimed me for lifetimes.

Alejandro, who carried me when I could not walk.

My daughters Adele and Juliet,
who made me a mother again.

Mom and Dad who patiently kept the light on.

Ronnie and William, who came to get me
but were not afraid to let me go.

FOREWORD

I ALWAYS KNEW I WANTED to be a mother. I come from a close-knit Jewish family in which nothing is more important than the children. After several early miscarriages, fertility treatment, burying twin girls miscarried at six months, and cancer, my husband and I finally had two healthy boys—Alec, my bright, verbal, redhead born through surrogacy, and Asher, my blond, Buddha-baby born after a surprising, high-risk pregnancy.

For a while, life was buoyant, productive and full of boy things. Thomas the Tank Engine, fishing and duck ponds, hide-and-seek through our dream house in the Arizona foothills. My husband and I were flourishing in our careers. Andre was a successful salesman, first of watches, then of real estate. I worked as a clinical director in a psychiatric emergency room, trying to keep people safe in their most perilous times. It was vital, rewarding work.

But over the course of the next few years, Andre came to reveal one dark secret after another, always followed by a desperate apology and promise to reform. Prostitutes, drinking, gambling in the form of day-trading away our savings. The only thing that seemed unequivocal was his devotion to the children. Eventually I filed for divorce, the two of us preparing to share custody of the boys across a bitter divide.

Then, on March 31, 2010, at 8:04 in the morning, my soon to be ex-husband shot and killed our two children:five-year-old Alec and fifteen-month-old-Asher.

For nearly four years, I have been living with this... this *what?* This fact. This tragedy, this shock, this loss, this aching. This emptying out of life as I knew it. But also, this other side, this hope, making a new life built on the only thing it can be: love.

This story is mine to live. No way around it.

It is also mine to tell.

The murders and Andre's subsequent death sentence received extensive coverage in the national and Arizona media. I turned down initial requests for interviews because I had nothing more to offer besides the terrible facts and a shocked numbness. Stunned, dazed, I waited each day for the kids to come home, for the morning to dawn differently, with my boys playing or sleeping in the next room.

In those early days, I developed something of a plan, a humble one that was all I could manage at the time: I was going to live until the murder trial was over. Then I was going to disappear. Not kill myself, exactly, but drift off and join my kids. It was as far as I could see, but it would get me through.

It did, some days better than others. Over time, through the love of family and friends, blinding moments of revelation, and the long, hard slog of grief and healing, I feel that I have gained perspective. I have begun to build a platform for living and embraced a role helping others find their way through grief, as a social worker specializing in counseling bereaved parents.

Now it is time to tell my story.

When I taped a recent episode of the *Dr. Phil* show, which aired in November, I was encouraged by the overwhelming response of the studio audience and of the wider audience tweeting during taping. They seemed to find inspiration in my story, that I survived the worst tragedy a mother can imagine and have gone on to live my life, share my story, help my clients, and even love and marry again (this news drew an eruption of applause from the studio audience).

It was the Fall, 2014, as I poured through emails from other parents, sisters, siblings, children, when my husband Alejandro made a request, an offering: "I've thought a lot about what is next for us, we need to share, I need to share you with the world and you need to share your teachings with them. You need to give it to them Beth, how you did it, how you made it back. The book is already written and lives inside of you, you just need to put it on paper", Alejandro said. He never does anything without thinking it through thoroughly, so I knew this was a well-formed proposal. "You have always been a mother, now you will parent, nurture and guide those who are lost to find their way home".

Those who I have had the privilege to counsel tell me that I am really good at death, but on the contrary, I think I am really great at living. My contribution comes from others giving me permission to step into such a sacred space, the transition from their life as they knew it into a new life, a different life after their favorite person has passed on. It is me who is grateful to be asked to teach others how to walk out of this place called hell on earth and journey back to a new life. I know this journey, being dropped into an unwanted, unexpected reality with no compass, no guide, just an instinct to live and a desire to return *home*, whatever or wherever that place may be, but all of us have one and seek it. For me, it was a place without suffering.

It was a next chapter, a new chapter—a new life, a family that builds on all that's come before and becomes something else entirely. What that is, I do not yet know. But, for the first time in seven years, I am exhilarated at the prospect of sharing my journey with others and embracing this life that was so perfectly recycled for me.

One last detail of the crime still lingers, Andre remains on death row. What is my position on his death? Will I attend the execution? Or not? How will I live my life and teach others to love themselves only through the ability to resolve resentment, anger, regret and embrace forgiveness but at the same time agree with an equally horrific act? Or are the two acts mutually exclusive? I believe it will be revealed, in its own time through my writings, how I will feel about a man who I once loved and who I claimed as my family, now a murderer of my children and who will be murdered himself.

ABOUT THE BOOK

Bulletproof goes behind the headlines to tell the before-during-and-after story of an unthinkable family tragedy. The book begins with a marriage like many other marriages, launching with love and arcing into family. Andre held my hand and made me laugh through infertility, a traumatic miscarriage, cancer, then the miraculous births of Alec and Asher. He taught me how to put on a diaper. He lay on the living room floor to set up Thomas's train tracks. He volunteered at the temple school as a "Shabbat dad." He took Alec fishing, brought the boys to feed the ducks at the golf course pond and watch the giant fish at the Bass Pro Shop.

Bulletproof will follow the marriage as it hit rocky shoals and ran aground. Dark secrets began to emerge. Andre visited prostitutes, even brought them to our house. He drank too much (we were going through one Costco-sized Bombay Sapphire a week—about fifty shots' worth), had a DUI and his driver's license suspended, and later, blew our savings through risky day-trading.

Bulletproof tells the story, too, of a marriage unlike most any other, ending as it does in murder and death row. There is, of course, the question of why. He did it to punish me. Because I was leaving him. Because he was afraid I was going to move away and take the children. Because, somehow, he thought it was a good idea given how his life was going. Trying to assign rational thought is something that I, the police, my family, the prosecutor, and the jury, have done countless times. But these attempts follow a path that never connects to the death of the boys. Rational explanation can never get anywhere near the killing, because it is the most irrational, unexplainable thing a father could ever do to his children.

Bulletproof will cover the trial, in which the Maricopa County Superior Court jury set an Arizona record for shortest deliberation in a murder trial. Eleven minutes. Guilty. And, less than forty-eight hours later, the sentence. Death. I have always been against the death penalty, but my beliefs are forever turned inside out. On death row, alone in a cell twenty-three hours a day and headed for execution, is someone with whom I chose to create a family. And the person who murdered my children.

Bulletproof will include stories from accident, to illness, to the myriad ways we can lose what we love most. In these sections, I will explore the infinite paths that we create to get back to ourselves and life here on earth when all we want to do is to follow our children to heaven.

The book will explore how relationship between mother and child continues after the death. I felt it first after a miscarriage at six months. Twin girls who were never born taught me about mothering. No, I never held them, cupped their downy heads, soothed their cries. Never even saw their faces. But we are forever linked in a primal bond. They first made me a mother. In an essential way, they also mothered me. Their induced, explosive delivery—during which I almost bled to death—exposed a cancer that had been nascent in me, revealed it to doctors in Stage I and quite possibly saved my life.

And the boys. I am still their mother, they are still my children. Perhaps, too, this one is now reversed. When I am at my lowest, when I feel like I am sleepwalking through life, it is Alec I pray to for strength and meaning. I'm not doing too well, Mumsie, I'll say. And I'll hear his familiar voice, his familiar phrase, "It's okay, Mom, it's okay." Over six years, I often watched my speedy adventurer and thought, "That boy's everywhere." Now he truly is. Hand-in-hand with Asher, whom he always called "my baby," Alec surrounds me. The two of them travel the universe, reporting back to me often and always coming when called, good boys that they are.

I have imagined a home for them—the tawny Arizona hills, the bright reds and purples of my garden. In the desert doves nesting on my back patio and, seven weeks later, baby chicks. I can see the children in anything cosmic, the dusty sweep of stars, the haloed moon, the stacked cumulonimbus clouds that herald desert rains. Home to them, this is also home to me. A world beyond this world and, at the same time, of this world. It is a borderland we both live in, I on this side, they on the other.

I have two homes: the uncontained universe where the boys are, which will always feel like home to me; and a Spanish-style stucco house in Scottsdale where I live with my husband and two stepdaughters, a koi pond out back and a Buddha garden in the side yard. *Bulletproof* will explore this life as a dual citizen and the challenge that lies in navigating the two worlds—as it has for the seven years and now.

About the Author

L AURIE BETH MORALES has unusual insight into loss and healing as both someone who has suffered the death of her two sons and a licensed clinical social worker specializing in grief and loss, including infertility, chronic and terminal illness, palliative care and end-of-life counseling. She has a psychotherapy practice in Scottsdale, Arizona, runs the Center for Palliative Counseling, and is a provider resource for the National Organization of Parents of Murdered Children, working with grieving parents from across the country. She has a Bachelor's Degree in Psychology and a Master of Social Work Degree from Arizona State University; has national certification in treating addictions; is a member of the Arizona Board for the Certification of Addiction Counselors; and has been in practice for more than twenty years. Since she has decided to tell her story publicly, she has appeared on *Dr. Phil* and her podcast reached #3 for mental health podcasts with Psych Sessions.

She lives in Scottsdale with her husband and two daughters.

MATCHMAKER

Think of all the beauty still left
around you and be happy.

- Anne Frank

"IT'S 4:06 PM, I have plenty of time", I thought to myself as I gave my last patient a hug and reminded her of her homework for the upcoming session. "Be well Kate, remember, you are brilliantly free when you are living your life in truth, without the story, see you in 2 weeks". I sat down to chart and reflect on my session, same place, different details. Noticing. Adapting. Moving. It's a miracle how far she has come, she has traveled a million miles since we first started our journey together, her brave trek out of Antarctica, as I refer to it.Look at her recovering from the death of her daughter. What a harsh story of self conviction, to believe that she was somehow responsible for the death of her daughter. An account that started so innocently, as do many of my patients' stories. It was a normal day, same routine as she did for the past 7 months. She put Baby Ali down for a nap, there were a few minutes of crying and cooing like she always did, but then quiet, she was asleep. Any Mom can relate to the welcoming sigh of a moment's peace for yourself before the next shift filled with diaper changes, feedings and Baby Einstein videos to stimulate that growing little mind. When she walked in 20 minutes later to check on her, she was dead. Gray. Lifeless. CPR was 15 minutes too late. Caught between the crib and the crib bumper. I remember what master belief resonated in her head as she sobbed session after session, torturing her every waking moment: "I bought that crib set, I wanted that crib set because I wanted everything to match and look beautiful, how stupid of me, instead of keeping her safe, it killed her;I killed her. Why didn't I know? I should have known. I'm the Mom, I was supposed to protect her". How does anyone walk out of that story, and not only live, but experience joy and happiness again? She was a miracle and so is her courage.

"4:15 pm, I have to go". I run inside the house, quickly change into a white cotton tee, black leggings and riding boots, kiss the cats , grab my bag and I'm off. L.A., here I come. Alejandro was so wild about this trip, I can't understand why he was so insistent on going to the consulate now, his Colombian passport doesn't expire for another 2 months. Oh well, I'll go with his flow, it'll be a fun get away weekend with my honey in Santa Monica;certainly no one needs to convince me to escape the Phoenix heat in August.

Good planning girl, I left myself plenty of time, after all, it was way too ambitious to think that I could catch the 4:58 flight, no way. I hopped on the freeway. No traffic. Strange, where is everyone on a Friday at 4:30 in the afternoon? What a gift, I'll take it. As I pull into the airport parking garage, schhwing! The first space in front is open. Nice, gift #2. If it's this easy, I should go to LA more often. Just as I was getting off the escalator, the Air Train pulls up, sweet. "OK, I am definitely buying a lottery ticket tonight", I thought to myself. This is too good to be true, but I am sure my lucky streak will run out when I get to security. One word: TSA. To my surprise, there was no line. OK, this is just freaky but I'm not going to look a gift horse in the mouth. "4:48". I looked at the monitor, "Maybe I *could* catch the earlier flight and surprise Alejandro?". "Gate C2. It's right there. I'm going for it".

"Can I still get on this flight to Los Angeles?"

"Do you have any checked bags?"

"No".

"You have to ask her, she's the boss", as the Southwest employee pointed to her coworker standing at the gate door.

I ran.

"Can I get on this flight?"

"You need to ask her", as she pointed back to the desk.

"Please, can I get on?" I asked as I ran back.

"Let me see if there's a seat. Usually it would cost you $138.00 and we close the doors in 1 minute".

" It's your lucky day, if she says you can board, I have the last seat for you".

I looked back at the gate with my hands clutched in a begging position.

"Come on girl!", she replied.

"Yes!" I shouted as she handed me my boarding pass.

Thank God I'm not wearing heels, I would have broken my ankle by now.

"Thank you so much, can I give you a hug?", I asked as she took my boarding pass.

"Why sure! Have a good flight sweetheart".

With that, the entire waiting area starting clapping. Unbeknownst to me, they were watching this demonstration of a human tennis match, airline style.

"4:53. I made it. Unbelievable", I thought to myself as I ran down the jetway. I have no idea how the universe calculated this one, but everything was orchestrated perfectly.

"12B". Here I am. I didn't care if I was scrunched in the middle, I was on the plane.

"Wow, that was close", he said.

"Yeah, the universe is definitely on my side with this one", I replied.

I closed my eyes with a smile on my face and thought of how surprised Alejandro would be when I show up at the hotel an hour early.

"Your smiling, you seem like such a happy person, especially for someone who almost had to run down the runway after the plane".

'Thank you, it's a miracle that I made it. I was supposed to catch the 6:10 flight because I had patients up until 4:00."

"What brings you to L.A.?", he asked.

" I'm surprising my honey, he flew out yesterday to get his Colombian passport renewed, so we decided to hit two birds with one stone and make a mini vacation out of it; no kids, no decision making, no appointments, just bikes on the beach, great food and weather that doesn't resemble Hades.

"Sounds like a great weekend. Colombian huh?", he asked.

"Yes, I love Latin men, Colombians especially.

"I get it, I'm Hispanic", he said.

"Then I don't need to explain further. I love the culture, the foods, the spicy machismo, the music, and definitely the way those hips move when they dance. Growing up in Miami, Florida made me fall in love with it all, and lucky me, I managed to find the only Colombian in probably all of Arizona".

Little did I know that I was sitting next to the first Hispanic American and first Gay American to serve two senior executive roles in the White House. Like I need to tell him about the allure of Hispanic culture?

"I'm Moe".

"Nice to meet you Moe, I'm Laure Beth. What are you heading to L.A. for?"

" Well, I have a book that is being published and I am going out there to meet with some people and discuss what's next".

"What's the book about?", I asked.

"Well, it's about a Hispanic boy, growing up in a small town in Texas who has a secret".

"I think that I know his secret", I whispered.

"You do?".

"Um hmm, he likes Latin men as much as I do".

We busted up laughing, giggling like two schoolmates in the library.

I have no idea what is happening but there is an instant connection with us, it's as if we have known each other for years. I know that sometimes people act strange on planes, maybe it's the subconscious thoughts about leaving the ground or fear of dying or maybe we know that we can say whatever we want to this person next to us because chances are, we will never see them again.

"I can't wait to read it, what's it called?".

"Little Secret, Big Dreams", as he reached in his carry-on bag to show me the cover.

"That must have been such a painful inner experience...gay, catholic, Hispanic and in Texas, hiding, wishing so badly to be able to tell someone but fearing the worst if you did."

"I don't understand the cover though?".

"Well, my story is about adversity, perseverance and survival when everything you know and love tells you that who you are is wrong. What I didn't tell you is that I was able to use all of my energy towards my American dream; I am the first Hispanic American and first Gay American to serve two senior executive roles in the White House."

" Amazing. You made it out, you got out of the shame, out of the shadows of the beliefs of who you are or aren't supposed to be. You had to get out or should I say, *come* out.

«Touché", Laurie Beth.

" And to end up at the White House serving our Vice Presidents Gore and Biden?! See, Latin men, so spicy, it's in your blood".

"I am writing a book too", I said.

"Really, what's it about?".

Oh God, OK Laurie, keep it together, this flight is only 51 minutes. No tears. Deep breath, here it goes...

" Six years ago, my two sons died. Killed. They were 5 years old and 15 months".

Silence.

"What can I get you to drink?", the flight attendant asked.

Great timing. It's was like when a server asks you how your meal is when you just put food in your mouth.

"Water please". "Me too".

"OK, now what!? How? Oh my God. How are you even here? And look at you, you bounce on this plane with a smile on your face. Who would have had any idea", Moe asked.

"I know. And there's more. It's so much bigger than that. Too much for a 51 minute plane ride".

"More? You mean there's more that has happened?!", Moe gasped.

"Yes, I've been told that I've won the suffering sweepstakes. I don't see it that way. My book is about adapting. Adapting to death. Loss. Reconstruction. But it's not only discussing pain, it's about becoming a Phoenix that rises from the ashes, from the destruction of everything that you know that tethers you to the earth. It's about learning how to live a new life, a different life because I can't live the same life that I was living: it's gone. And trying to live the same life that I was, to put it simply, is painfully unbearable. That's the only reason why I chose *this* way, is because I don't want to hurt. The moment that I heard they were dead, *that* life vanished and I was given a life in trade that was indistinguishable. No identity. No name, no home, no family. No direction. Antarctica. Left only with a beating heart that I wished many a nights that it would stop."

"Oh my God, but h*ow*? How do you do it?".

"Well, I guess you'll have to read my book. It's taken me almost seven years to get to this point, it lives inside of me, and will not be born before it's ready. It is not something that I am writing, it is already written, I am simply giving it the space to be witnessed.

That is what my book is about. It is learning how to adapt to the unthinkable and to live, but it's not enough to just survive. Living is a choice. And if I am here, choosing to live, I am going to have happiness. I will not live here and suffer, that is not an option *for me*. I do not see myself as injured, but I have sustained horrible injuries. That is what I have and I generously offer it to anyone who I am so fortunate enough to share the grains of sand in my hourglass with. I have to give it back."

"Yes, yes, but how did you get *here!?* And what is *it?* What is that "*it*" factor because this is like the holy grail that we all are searching for."

How *did* I get here? (Thinking to myself)…

PART ONE

SEPARATION

OUT OF BODY

I have loved the stars too fondly
to be fearful of the night.

- Galileo

MARCH 30, 2010:
He's getting so big, I thought, as I snuggled into the bean-bag with my son, my arm against the downy peach fuzz of his. Didn't I used to have more room here?

Five years old and feeling every ounce of it, Alec was considering our plans for the long weekend as his baby brother napped. "Not the children's museum," he said, articulating carefully because he was making a point. "That's for babies. I want to go to the science museum."

So the next day, Tuesday, March 30, 2010, we were off to the Arizona Science Center. There would be one more reminder in the car. "Remember, Mom. The science museum." For big kids; I get it. Kindergarten, apparently, can do this to a kid. I looked at the boys in the rearview mirror. Alec was starting to sprout, his features just beginning to sharpen. I was getting a hint of what was around the corner, the lean, gentle, milky-skinned young man he would become. He was bright and alert, always ready with a question or an answer. Or two. "We are going to the science museum, Mr. Chunkers." He reached over and squeezed Asher's Buddha thigh.

Once we arrived, Alec ran to the front door. Asher teetered behind, fistful of pretzel sticks in one hand, almost empty baggie in the other. For fellow travelers, which they were from beginning to end, they followed such different trajectories. Alec knew where he wanted to go, and he moved through space and time as efficiently as he could to get there. He was a bullet train. Asher was a meanderer. Walking, which he'd just recently mastered, was not a means to an end but an end in itself. He would follow Alec until he lost him, then he would just walk. Zigging and zagging, changing direction like (or with) the wind. Whenever we had a real destination, we traveled in some combination of walk, hand-holding and, finally, the scoop-up. Hoisting twenty-eight pounds of pure chunk and smile.

From the whooshing entry of the front door, the museum lived up to Alec's big-boy hopes and dreams:climbing ropes, bubbles, balloons, dinosaurs, gravity, outer space. He didn't know where to run first. Finally, those wide blue eyes landed on the Human Body exhibit, and he darted over to a group of kids gathered around an oversized human heart. He was just starting to make discoveries about the world inside himself. He knew he had a heart, and he had commented before about hearing my heart as he lay on my chest during tickle time. But he had never actively listened to his own.

The exhibit educator was asking for volunteers, and Alec, as usual, thrust his hand in the air. "I'm Alec, A-L-E-C," he said when called on.

The task at hand couldn't have been more perfect for him. Run around the table five times as fast as you can.

As he sprinted and Asher sat contentedly with his pretzel sticks, I thought: no matter how bitter the divorce swirling around them, we were managing to build an oasis around the kids. They loved Mommy, Daddy, and each other. They loved school, gymnastics, their friends, Grandma and Grandpa. They had a familiar comfortable spot, our old house, with Andre. And, with me, they were starting a new home. A small cottage house with a courtyard for them to play. Bit by bit, we were making it ours, with Buzz Lightyear bedsheets, Asher's pack'n'play crib, Alec's trains and budding egg collection. A friend with a farm had even showed up with an emu egg. We were starting to build collections, memories, and train paths through made-up towns. The new house was all right with Asher because I had brought with us his favorite possession in the world: the blow dryer. It was his own private Caribbean vacation, warm breeze across his face. And the house was all right with Alec. He had been asking, "Why can't we all go home, Mama?" Avoiding the ugliness for the moment, I told him a white lie. "This house is closer to my work at the hospital," I said. "So it's easier for me to help people."

This got him right in his empathic soft spot. "No problem," he said. "We gotta help people."

Back at the museum, Alec was being outfitted with a stethoscope. "Mom, I hear it!" he called, brimming with the discovery of his body's engine, now thundering from all that running. "Come here, listen to my heart."

Even though I had heard his heartbeat many times before, from those early ultrasounds that proved his existence, I was reassured by that loud lub-dub. He is here. He is strong.

We had lunch on the lawn outside the museum. I set up our picnic of hotdogs and chips, first Asher's, then Alec's. Then mine—but where was my hotdog? I checked the cooler, the grass around us. No hotdog. When in doubt, check Asher. There he sat, eating hotdogs double-fisted. "That's our Buddha baby," I said, rescuing what was left of my lunch. Alec, big brother, smiled at his baby, and Asher took it all in his usual stride. It is a simple image, a picnic on the grass in the hot sun with my boys before I returned them to their father that afternoon, the choreography of joint custody. It is an image that should have been one of countless memories, unremarkable and overtaken week by week, year upon year, with another happy moment, another picnic, another adventure, another childhood discovery.

Seven o'clock in the morning, Wednesday, March 31. My cell phone rings. Andre. I'm not answering it. It's too early for one more vindictive battle, yet another demeaning exchange.

"What time is it?", I asked Alejandro as I leaned over and laid on his back. Gosh, I am in heaven, I thought as he held me in his arms.

"Seven, OK, let's get up, you have your boys tonight and I have the girls, so let's do this so we can get out of the hospital at a decent time". I reached over to kiss him once again, "I like you Laurie Beth, just a little bit", he said. I fell back on the pillow and smiled. I wasn't planning on meeting someone, especially since the dust hasn't yet settled with the "King of France", that's what I refer to my soon-to-be ex-husband Andre. I had to find some way to make reference to him when I am in the presence of Alec and Asher, so I could shelter them, as much as I can, from the unfortunate ugliness of divorcee communication. Even through all of the chaos of moving out, lawyers, new bank accounts, and adapting to this 50/50 custody thing, I found a pocket of paradise.

My cell phone rings. Andre. I'm not answering it. It's too early for one more vindictive battle, yet another demeaning exchange. Two minutes later, the phone rings again. Stop call—

It's not him, it's my neighbor on East Cactus Wren Road. I pick up. "Laurie, what the hell is going on at your house?" she says, meaning where Andre now lives. "It's surrounded by a SWAT team. Helicopters are everywhere."

I can barely breathe as I call the school. Please... please... please let the kids be there. They are not.

I race to my car, race to East Cactus Wren Road. The subdivision's guardhouse is swarming with police. Maybe he killed himself. Please, God, let my children be okay.

"I have the mother coming back," a police officer radios on his walkie-talkie.

The house is barricaded. SWAT teams prowl. More police officers, more firepower than I've ever seen in one place. They let me as far as my girlfriend's house, the friend who called me. Across the street and two doors down from my babies. I am met by two police officers in her garage.

"Laurie, honey, Alec and Asher have been hurt," my friend tells me.

"Are they okay?" I ask.

I want desperately to know.

I don't want to know.

"No, honey. They are dead."

I beat on the police officer's chest. To beat the words away. Beat the facts away. My children are lying alone, inside a crime scene. I must get them out. This protective impulse—I am a mother—is primal. It is nature, and it impels me. It has no outlet—I cannot get to them—and it tingles my fingers and my spine.

I just heard that telltale heartbeat. Just yesterday.

Everything is off its axis. I want to lie down and never wake up. I want to run and never stop. My world is split, shattered, moving everywhere at once. Moving nowhere. Stuck in sludge. So this is what they mean by an out-of-body experience.

"What about Andre?" I ask. Not that I fucking care.

"He tried to shoot himself but botched it. He is being taken to the hospital. He is alive and just blew off some of his cheek". Just stop. I don't care. I don't fucking care.

The police will not let me go to the house. They do not want me to see the children like this. I want to see them, I can't leave them. I can't see them like this, whatever this is. If I do, I will never be able to get the image out of my brain. But I can't leave them. I looked at the house. "They are all alone, lying over there, alone, murdered, alone and I can't go". What the hell do I do? Oh God, please help me, help me, please, I don't know what to do. I can't do this. I am quickly escorted into Wendi's house. An officer takes my cell phone. They question me about the shooting. About Andre, about the divorce, about his relationship with the children, my relationship with the children. A gun, did I know he had a gun?

Alejandro asks permission, first from me, then from the police, to go into the house, to make sure that Alec and Ashie are not alone. That they know their mama is here.

Where is here? How can I be so deeply with them and so unbearably far from them? I long to hold them and tell them it's going to be okay. But it's not going to be okay. It's never again going to be okay. Never.

After hours of this—two, three, five hours?; that day has been unloosed from time—I just want to go home. Bone-deep, gut-deep, all I want to do is go home.

But I have no home to go to. Where do I go? There is no place to call home. Across the street, once my home, is where my boys have just been killed. I cannot go home to the little cottage house that the boys and I have been slowly transforming into ours, with trains, eggs, Buzz Lightyear. That would be impossible. My nascent life there is vanished. I would step right off the edge of the earth if I stepped across that threshold.

I don't even know who I am. Laurie Leteve. I cannot bear that name, his last name, which I've had for eleven years.

I have no children.

I have no home.

I have no name.

It is finally decided (I say it like this because all my agency is gone and I can decide nothing; things get decided) that I will go to Alejandro's house. Helicopters are circling; media are swarming; rubberneckers are rubbernecking. I crouch on the backseat floor of Alejandro's car, someone's jacket over my head. I am being smuggled out. I am a fugitive. On the run from a horrible crime. My life, in an instant, has become a horrible crime.

Four o'clock. Somehow, it has become four o'clock. Pick up, the computer calendar alerts, cruelly catching my attention. There I see my life. Friday, Passover carnival. Sunday, play date with Zach. April 3, return library books.

Passover carnival. Delete.

Playdate on Sunday. Delete.

Library. Delete.

Pick up at 4. Delete. Delete. Delete.

This is just the beginning of the phantom-limb pain to come. Infinite pain that forever seeks a locus and the locus is no longer here. So the pain can never land, never root. Never go away.

When I finally drift off to sleep, I wake up leaking tears, oozing them. There is nothing conscious to this act, no, something sad happened and I will cry. It is wholly involuntary. I can no more control shedding tears than you could control bleeding from an unstaunched wound. I open my eyes hoping that this is just a dream, please let it be a dream. I turn over on Alejandro's bed, the same bed that I dreamed in less than 24 hours ago was now supporting me in my worst nightmare. I am hollowed.

My family is flying in. My parents from Florida, my brother, aunts, uncles, and cousins from New York, my sister and her family. As soon as I collapse into a hug with my Dad, to whom I've always looked for answers, I realize that no one, not even he, can guide me. Take my hand and walk… Pump your legs and swing… Follow my finger and read… Here's how you find a job… get married… change a diaper… discipline a child… Of all the things parents, siblings, lovers, mentors and teachers can help us do in our lives, this one is a stumper. How do you carry on living when your estranged husband murders your children? There are no lessons in life to ramp you up for that one.

Over the next several days, I sit Shiva. It's more than sitting Shiva: I sit. That is all that I can do. Sit. I can't seem to do anything else, it is all so bitter and painful. Being here, not there. Them not being here. All that brings me comfort right now is to look at their pictures, I have them stacked across Alejandro's fireplace mantle, and I sit. People come to me, I really don't move a lot. They make me bites to eat, all trying to comfort themselves by comforting me; it's not working. I tell everyone to not talk to me when I am trying to eat because it just makes me want to cry. Do you know how hard it is to eat when you are crying? Try it one time, it's impossible. I plan a funeral. I sign the burial papers after carrying them around for two days. How can a mother sign such a thing? Through my rabbi I petition the Rabbinical Society for cremation (they assent), as it is against Jewish law.

I am supposed to be getting the children ready for school, discussing with Alec which song we would sing in the car. Instead, I am choosing music for the memorial service: their favorite, "Little Wonders" from Meet the Robinsons. I close my eyes—to block the image or call it up?—and I can see their bopping heads so clearly. Little boys, catchy song. Our lives are made in these small hours, these little wonders, the twists and turns of fate.

My rituals were supposed to be nothing more, and nothing less, than gathering today's outfits, laid out the night before. Making buttered toast for Alec's breakfast, cereal and fruit for Asher. Bagging lunches and snacks, sliced salami, grapes and Goldfish. And out the door at 7:45 for preschool.

Instead of these treasured rituals, I am making known my wishes to have the boys wrapped together for cremation, along with Alec's favorite stuffed animal, Cow Cow. This worn cow-headed blanket had been with him all his life. I had a police officer retrieve it from the crime scene, and I've held onto it ever since, as Alec used to do in babyhood. I've been sleeping with it. It still smells like him.

"Laurie, they are bringing Alec's Cow Cow over,". Oh my God, they got his Cow Cow. This was the fastest that I have moved in days since my babies died. I opened the door, it was a man from our Temple who volunteered to retrieve it from the police, he handed it to me, crying

" My son died too, I wanted to be the one to bring this to you".

I hugged him and we held each other for some time, it was as if he wanted to say how sorry he was for being in "his club" now.

"Detective Lockerby wanted me to give you a message...he said to tell you that Alec had Cow Cow, he was holding him".

Alec's favorite stuffed animal. This worn cow-headed blanket had been with him all his life. My only request was to have the police retrieve it from the crime scene. They found it, it was just as Alec had it. It still smells like him. I'm never going to let it go, just like Alec.

What do you call a parent anyway who's children dies? If my spouse dies, I would be a widower, if it was my parents, I would be an orphan, but what am I, what does that make me now? Am I a Mom if I don't have kids? Who am I if there is no word in the English language for a mother with deceased children? Or maybe there is, maybe it's not a noun but an adjective; broken, empty, alone. And do I say that I have kids anymore? What do I say? I have kids, I don't have kids and if I say I have kids, then how old are they? Where are they? Of course I have kids, I will never say that I don't, that would be erasing them, making them disappear. No, I claim them and they claim me. Forget that; my kids may be dead but I will never deny them or separate from them, ever.

I ran upstairs, Alejandro in tow, he just signaled for everyone to stay back. I just held Cow Cow as I dove into Alejandro's bed, weeping from the bowels of my soul. It smelled like Alec, that was my Alec. Like a wounded animal, at that moment, death would be welcomed and seen as an act of compassion to relieve my suffering.

"I want him back, please, I just want him back", I bellowed. I can't handle this, I just know that I can't handle this, this is a fucking nightmare. I want to go home, I just want to go home.

I knew what that meant, on so many different levels but I couldn't decode that, not now.

"Laurie, baby, we have to talk about what you want to do with the babies", Alejandro said as he stroked my hair.

"I want them back. I want them back. That's what I want to do, I want to get them back. I want to hold them and give them a bath, I want to have a pillow fight, I want to make Alec cinnamon toast like he ate every morning, I want to see Asher demand my hair dryer when I am blow drying my hair, I want to watch Thomas the Train videos and set up train tracks, I want it all back, that's what I want to do with the boys".

"I know my love, but we don't get that", he said tearfully.

What to do with my babies? I was supposed to be going to Peter Piper Pizza tonight with them, that's what I'm supposed to be doing with them.

" I need for you to sign these papers my love, the hospital needs to know where you would like to have the boys taken and if you would like to bury or cremate them".

That must have been one of the hardest things that Alejandro will ever have to do in his life, give a mother her children's death directives to execute. I got up off the bed and stood up to wash my face, afterwards returning to the bedroom where I asked to see the papers. I leaned up against the wall and slid down, looked at the papers as if they were death itself; the final order that I am tasked to execute, to destroy the remains of my two beautiful babies, those amazing little bodies that I worked so hard to create. Time did stand still, I couldn't tell you how long I sat there, there was no rush. Irreversible. Trauma is so crazy, I am somehow hoping that if I waited long enough, maybe, just maybe, they would come back, that someone would burst in the door and scream," Wait, don't do it, it was a mistake, they're alive!".

"Can you get my Dad", I asked.

"This is so weird and surreal, I'm calling my Dad to Alejandro's bedroom?", I thought to myself as my Dad entered. My father, my beacon for what is right, gently talks me into it. In the end, I know that Alec needs it more than I do. That's what a mother does, sacrifices for her children. It is one of life's most cherished privileges. Not only that. Judging by how tightly I was holding onto the stuffed cow, my father knows it could become an anchor that would sink me.

"Cremated. I want them to be cremated. I don't want them in a hole, with dirt on top of them. I want them to be with me, near me. I don't want to go to a place with visiting hours so I can be with them. I want to take them to Holland and spread them among the tulips, I want to take them to the snow, I want to share them with the world, and when people look at all of the beautiful places, I can smile, knowing that Alec and Asher are a part of that".

"That sounds nice Laurie, we will take care of it".

I signed the papers of destruction and handed them to Alejandro. I walked over to the bed and laid down with Cow Cow.

"Laurie Beth, you need to let Cow Cow go, let Alec have his Cow Cow".

God I could smell him, if I just closed my eyes, I could smell him and feel him, just like how I did 2 days ago. I never want to stop smelling him, but eventually I will, and that is going to be horribly painful.

"OK Daddy, I know he needs Cow Cow more than me, but I don't want to. I will but I don't want to. I just want them back and I want to go home".

He just held me and cried, he couldn't make it better, there was nothing to make it better. We were buried in grief and could not get air. I didn't want to let Cow Cow go, just like my Dad did not want to let me go, I was slipping away and he knew it, I had been pulled up by my roots, nothing was sufficient to ground me and there wasn't a damn thing he could do. I lost my kids and he saw that with every decision and every minute that went by, he was losing me.

I sign the burial papers after carrying them around for two days. How can a mother sign such a thing? It wouldn't be that easy. "I have about two thousand people rallying behind this mother, we need to support her and this congregation, this community that is standing behind her", Rabbi Linder proclaimed. He petitioned on my behalf to the Rabbinical Society for cremation (they assent), as it is against Jewish law and they listened, Alec and Ashie would stay with me.

"I can't do this, I can't be here, I can't be here", I said as I fell to my knees. "It's too much", I gasped to catch my breath. Get me the f**k out of here. " Laurie, tell me what you want, I'll get it baby, just wait in the car", Alejandro said as he led me away. "Alec's Thomas the Tank Engine shirt, his favorite matchbox car, it's shaped like a shark. I want his giraffe beanie baby and the beanie bear that says," MOM" and my orange ring. It's by the bedside. He'd recently given me on Purim. "Mama", he said, "You are more beautiful than Queen Esther", as he stood on the Bimah. It is as if it was yesterday. Wait a minute, it was yesterday. That's what happens when death stops life. Time stops. It doesn't matter how many days pass, it feels like yesterday. Everything I cherish and care about is now able to fit into a nightstand drawer.

I answer more questions from the police. Ask away, as if there is some answer out there that would help us understand why? The question

of course was asked if he had a mental illness. Just because he tried to commit suicide after the murders but failed by shooting himself through the chin doesn't make him crazy, just stupid. He was virulently angry at me, as always lately, and despondent over his mounting losses (family, finances) but ultimately his loss of control. His desperate attempts to get me back had failed, the begging , pleading or attempts to control me were not working. Andre began to up the ante. When he called the police on me, when he arbitrarily wanted me out of the house when I was going to bed one night, when he got in my face, pulled at my clothes and called me a whore when I was putting on lipstick as I was getting dressed to go to work. Sending flowers to a hospital administrator and signed them from Alejandro, as to try to get me fired for having a relationship with a physician. And when that failed, the ultimate chess move, so I thought, he petitioned the Court for emergency guardianship because he thought that I was apparently going to kidnap the children and move to Florida, although I am licensed in Arizona, have lived here for twenty-four years and have never had any plans to move. FAILED.

He didn't just snap. You can't be crazy and premeditate a crime, knowing right from wrong. He was pissed and full of vengeance. He had, it turned out, been planning this murder for weeks. He'd bought the gun, after a three-day waiting period, from the Bass Pro Shop, where we took the boys on leisurely weekends to feed the fish and tuck into a chicken-finger lunch. On his computer, investigators found several drafts of a murder-suicide note, written over several days. "Enjoy the rest of your life without us," the final note said. It was taped to the door, hand-written in a calm everyday script, as if it said, "Gone to the store to pick up some milk, be right back." He signed it "A" and had the children sign, too. My big boy, who just learned to write his name, proudly spelling out A-L-E-C for Daddy. And Asher, all fist, taking the pen and chicken-scratching away. How sick, he had them sign their own death note.

I hugged my babies, kissed them goodnight, put them to bed, fed them, took them to school—while their father was planning their murder?

MEMORIAL DAY

A conditional happiness dependent on any specific circumstances always leads to suffering.

- Dalai Lama

SUNDAY, APRIL 4, 2010:
Groundhog's Day. Not actually but it feels like it. I open my swollen eyes to look out the window, yes, another day is here and the reality that they are not. I had no idea that it was possible to cry when you are sleeping, but I can now attest to it. Alejandro turns me towards him , he strokes my hair as my tears fall onto his chest.

"I don't want to do this today". He just holds me and listens.

"Let's go walking", he said. This was our routine since we met 8 months ago. We loved walking together, we would walk everywhere, to dinner, to the grocery store, for ice cream, 3 miles, 5 miles, in the rain, it didn't matter. We would walk, hand in hand and just talk about everything and anything.

Asher, Adele, Juliet and Alec Matthew

It was perfect, he had kids, I had kids, they played together, all of our little ducks: Adele 5, Alec 4, Juliet 3 and Ashie 15 months, everything just fell into place, we even had the same parenting time schedule, then BAM! Oh God, how are we going to explain this to Adele and Juliet? What do we say happened to their friends? What can we say? I know what I don't want to say nor do I think any 6 and 4 year old should be exposed to hearing about: the ugly aspect of reality that children are murdered by their parent(s).

Later, this is too much. I can't think about this right now.

I brushed my teeth, got dressed and we were off. Walking is so metaphorical for my life right now, one foot in front of the other. One mile, two miles, three...if only I could walk away from this, walk backwards to somehow roll back time, to walk back to before all of this happened. I've always loved waking up and walking in the mornings, being the only one on the streets, watching the sun come up, gently lifting the spell of sleep. Now I hate it. Dawn is just an invitation to another day without my boys. No thanks, I'll pass.

I am not sure if he has ever been around that many people from Long Island or Westchester, but New York Jewish is a different animal in and of itself, and my loving herd was on their way. I had to orient Alejandro to my family and the cultural invasion that was about to arrive.

All of the sudden, I notice that a red cardinal is following us and I mean following us. Not for one or two minutes, but for the entire walk. I stopped. to acknowledge his presence as he sat on a limb of a Palo Verde tree.

"Hi. I see you. Can you see me? I'm here."

I just continued to stare at this beautiful bird. I could feel the sun was shining in my face and a cool breeze. So this is where you live now? This is how you will come to me?

Now I know that I have not lost my mind, I am not a crazy, spiritual person with crystals and patouhuli oil and thank God Alejandro was witnessing this as well, or I might have believed that I was going insane. I know that my children did not reincarnate into a bird. It is such a comforting thought though, that the only way that this master spirit of energy can communicate to and with me is through symbols. It doesn't have a language, a mouth, a brain, a body to communicate with this human body, so symbols are what we have to connect with.

I am clear. I am going to speak at the service. I have to do this. I am their mother, how could I not speak and share with everyone just how great my children are? I am a mom, a parent. It is my responsibility to send a message and set the tone for how we will be, to shepherd us all in a direction of love and to not give this senseless act of hate any credence. My girlfriends get me ready, they try their best to keep me upbeat, but no amount of makeup can cover up the grief, for any of us.

Easter Sunday. 1 p.m. That is when I memorialize my kids, send them to the side of God. How ironic, just like another who came before who marked this holy day. The condolence line stretches outside and around the block. About eight hundred people are here. I am surrounded by huge poster boards of Alec and Asher. This is a dream. An episode of Law and Order. Someone else's life. Alejandro quickly guides me into the Temple and I am sequestered in the Rabbi's office with my immediate family. I feel sick, I want this to go away but it is inextricably soldered in me. The Rabbi asked if he could meet with me alone, we went outside in a private garden.

"Is there anything else that I can do for you or the boys? Please let me know".

"You are the closest one to God, can you ask him to bring them back?".

He held my hand and we cried together, feeling powerless, knowing that it doesn't work like that.

"Make sure that Traci is sitting with us", I requested. Traci, my angel. She was my surrogate in carrying Alec. She helped me become a Mom. She needs to sit in the front row, she earned that position.

It's time. As I walk down the aisle, I feel eyes on me, eyes of pity, horror, pain, disbelief, sadness, admiration. Just a week ago,

I was here, in the sanctuary, celebrating Purim with Alec. That was so much fun, he asked me to make him a cape for the Purim parade. Alec was so clear on what he had wanted the cape to look like: red on the outside, white on the inside and his name on the back, in big, blue letters. That was such a fun day, he was asked to join the Rabbi on the bimah to say a prayer, he raised the wine cup (filled with grape juice of course), turned around and looked at me and said,"L'Chaim Mom". Tears fall like drops of rain on my lap as I look at the ring he had given me from his Purim party bag, it was a butterfly, orange of course. His favorite color. "You are more beautiful than Queen Esther". And now, I am here, in the same place, attending his funeral? I look up and there are Alec and Ashie's pictures, blown up, life size on the Bimah.

"When were these pictures taken? I have never seen them.", I ask.

"Those are pictures the school took of Alec and Asher for Mother's Day", whispered Alejandro.

I just smiled. Mother's Day. That was my favorite, the most important day for me of the year, more than any day, that was the day that I became a Mom. Deleted. Now it's a day that will haunt me forever, to serve as a reminder that my mothership was taken away. Is there any way to hide from that day? Is it even possible?

Alec was so proud of his cape

I speak at the service because I can't not speak. I cannot not talk about my children, I need to breathe them back into life in this room, sear them into memory, into the walls, into the souls of my family and friends and neighbors overfilling the temple. Can I get another twenty, thirty minutes with my kids through sheer force of memory?

Alec celebrating Purim: L'Chaim!

Let the procession begin. First up, my niece, next Aunt Blossom and Uncle David, followed by my sister Ricki and her husband Topher. Last before me, my Dad and Mom. OK here I go. As I walk up to the podium, I hear whispers and undertones from the congregation," She's speaking? Look at her, how is she doing it?"I looked down and took a deep breath. What is that? A purple, velvet bag. Wait, is it? Oh my God, that's them! Calm Laurie, calm. It is surreal, I am looking at my children reduced into the compartment of a bag? I can't look down, I can't look at the bag. It is too much, my brain cannot wrap itself around that. Too painful. Calm. Calm. I take a deep breath. I have to do this. Here I go. I can do this. I look out into the sea of distraught faces, sitting on the edge of their seat, as if they were waiting to hear God Himself. Waiting to understand, waiting to somehow gleam a morsel of sense or peace out of this wreckage, waiting to hear where we go from here now. I am clear that I don't have anyone's answers, I only have the task of finding mine. There is no person, preparation, or go-to guide to help me know what I should do or how to be where I am at this moment in time, but I am clear, that the answers for me are within me, not *out there*. I don't know what to say or what now lives inside of me, and I may never understand or have answers, it may take the rest of my life to find them, but I know that there is something within me that is demanding to be brought into the sunlight and to be witnessed. I have something to say. It is unconscionable as a parent to eulogize your child, no matter what the age is. It is the ultimate in painful decisions that one has to make, but it is also a very clear decision. They belong to me and it is my responsibility and honor to tell you just how wonderful these two boys are.

My Boys: Alec and Asher

EULOGY:

Many of you know, that I am a private person, but for you to know about my boys, I will have to open my kimono with love and trust and share with you...

I sought my education, I sought my love and felt complete, the only desire left was to be a mommy. After many years of trying to have a baby, I became pregnant with twins. I lost them at 6 months precipitously. Six months following, I was diagnosed with Hodgkin's Lymphoma. I was lost. Many years followed. I am alive. My lesson: I am not afraid to die, I am afraid to not love.

So back to wanting to be a Mommy. The doctors said it was not safe to get pregnant. I turned to my Mom , as moms make everything better and she said," So we will have someone carry our baby for us". And that is what we did. A beautiful angel of a woman carried our Alec. The doctors were naysayers, "Don't get your hopes up", they would say, "This usually doesn't work". They didn't know us. Traci turned to the doctor and said," You just do your thing, I'll take care of the baby". We got pregnant on the first try.

Alec was the perfect pregnancy until he decided, as his spirit defines, that he is coming. He was 6 weeks premature. I was working at the psychiatric emergency at the time, I ran off the unit screaming, "I'm going to have a baby!". The patients took one look at me and thought that I was crazy. I flew to Albuquerque and upon my arrival, I started heading towards the little Hispanic baby with brown hair. To my surprise, that was not my baby, mine was the little strawberry blonde.

So let me share with you about Alec:

1. Two words, Red head. Alec was a gingy, he thought for a while that his first name actually was Gingy. In Israel, they say that God made gingies with special souls, that is how he can detect them amongst us. Whenever we would go out and he would be complimented on his beautiful red hair, he would respond and say, "Thank you, but my hair is orange, not red". He was so spicy, he definitely had a mind of his own, he was never disrespectful or defiant, he just knew at the young age of 5 his truth and how to honor himself. One time in school, his class was participating in a doll dress up activity, Alec was having nothing to do with that. The teacher asked if he wanted to go sit in the front office with Mrs. Marianne, and he accepted. He spent the next hour helping Mrs. Marianne greet people, organize her desk and made sure she knew when it was time for him to return to his class so he could play, but not before the doll playing was over. When he would get cross with me, he would say, "Mom, you are so fired!". What an amazing sense of self.

Alec's space helmet

2. Thomas the Train: He knew every train's name, color and personality. He was fascinated with trains, we would spend hours building tracks all over the house. As a parent, you would do anything for your kids, and man, did I ever. I must have listened to every Thomas the Train song known to man. But I loved doing it because it brought joy to Alec and I was so happy to be part of that. Don't get me wrong, I was really happy when Alec transitioned from Thomas to Hot Wheels, what would I give now to hear those train songs again with him.

3. *Alec had emotional intelligence. He knew when it was Mommy and Alec's time. Ashie would be put down for a nap or for the night and he had me all to himself. Our quiet time was of course, making train tracks and storytelling of the trains' adventures, coloring, playing the memory game, making brownies together, he even loved looking at the VS catalogues to give me his opinion on which bathing suit color he liked. One time, it was about 20 minutes after the three of us had woken, he turned to me and said,* " *Mommy, is it time for Asher's nap yet?*".

4. *Alec was wise and compassionate: He "saw" people. We "saw" each other. The delight I feel looking deep into Alec's pupils as if looking through a portal. "How do you know I love you?" I ask. "Because you see me, Mom," he would say. I remember how Alec made*

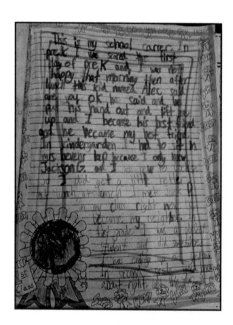

Zach's letter 4 years later: reflections of his friend Alec

a space helmet one day—all cardboard, pipe cleaner and imagination—and said, "Mom, will you take me to the moon?" How could I resist such an adventure with my favorite person? "Of course I will, Mumsie," I told him. I just didn't know that he would be going there first.

Whenever I was sad and he caught a tear in my eye, he would grab my face and say, " *It's OK Mom. I will get Zach and Holden (his friends) and tell them to be nice to you". When we were sitting in the oncology office waiting room, he got up and sat next to an older lady and just put his hand on her leg to comfort her. He was 4. I taught him, but he invariably knew, that what mattered was kindness. He perceptually knew how to be.*

5. *Alec was opinionated, very. If Alec thought that something was great, he wanted to share it with everyone. We had this huge lemon tree in our backyard, Alec loved to make lemonade. He asked me if he could teach his friends how to make lemonade, so that's what we did. He was so methodical when he presented it to his classmates: Step 1: Wash your hands. Step 2: Cut the lemon this way, not that way, and so on. Old soul.*

6. *Alec was a lover: He loved his baby brother. When Alec was about to turn 5 and we were discussing his birthday party, he made it clear that he wanted to have his party with Ashie (who turned 1 year just 11 days later), and out of all of his friends, he wanted Ashie to sit next to him. He loved his best friend Zach, Zach was diagnosed with autism at the age of 2 1/2, he was non-verbal, but that didn't stop Alec. They had their*

Zach's letter: A true expression of friendship

own language, we would watch them play and communicate in their own way for hours.

When Zach's parents were trying to potty train Zach, it was actually Alec who taught him through modeling on a picnic at the train park. "I'll show Zachy", he announced. And he did.

The years passed and life was beautiful. I am healthy. I am a Mommy. I have my Alec. Then one day, I was feeling ill. My first thought...it's back. I went to Dr. Ondreyco and she said, "I have

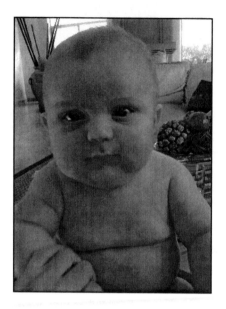

Asher Samuel

something to tell you. You are pregnant". Yes me, 2 1/2 months pregnant. All of the physicians were dumbfounded. So, in my fashion, as learned from Traci, I said to them," Just do your thing, I'll take care of the baby". We didn't tell Alec that we were pregnant, given our history, but one day, he came up to me and put his hands on my stomach and said, "Mommy, my baby's in here. He's here".

He knew, they were kindred souls, waiting to be reunited . Seven months later, Asher was here, so let me tell you about my Ashie...

1. *Asher was my Buddha Baby, he was 28 pounds and loved for me to carry him. When I couldn't carry him anymore, I would put him down and tell him that it was my turn. One time, when I put him down, he theatrically laid himself on the ground as to watch and wait for me to give in. I proceeded to lay down next to him and we just looked at each other. He seemed perplexed as to what was going on. Alec walked in on us and said," Mom, that's not a good idea". He was a Buddha, always smiling and easy going.*

2. *Did I mention that he loved to eat? On the first day of pre-school, I went to visit Asher to see how he was doing and to my surprise, all of the kids were crying, wanting to go home but*

there was Ashie, sitting at the table eating pancakes, probably thinking,” This place is great, I don't get it?”. Alec called him Mr. Chunkers. He loved stealing hotdogs off of our plates and would "do a little happy dance" while eating.

My boys only knew 2 things: that they were loved and that fun was the best thing to have.

If someone asked me if I wanted a gift, but the gift will have to be returned, would I still want it? I was given not one miracle, but two.

My answer is a resounding yes. The pain that I feel is only reflective of just how much I love them.

My boys

So now what? What does one do with a belief in miracles when the miracles are taken back? I feel like chicken little, I believe that the sky fell and the earth opened up. But the moral of chicken little is that the sky is not falling, but I'm not there yet.

Alec and Ashie will be where life is, not death. I want them to be part of creating life. I want to sprinkle them in the tulip fields in Holland, I want to plant them with our lemon tree, I want to sprinkle them on milkweed plants so they can make the journey with the Monarch butterflies. I want to learn how to live with them and without them. A tall order.

I have the best family and I am so grateful to be loved by you and to have you allow my boys and I to love you. I ask this of you when you go to sleep at night. Tell your babies that there are 2 angels that you have received lessons from today:

1. Just love. The opposite of love is not hate, but indifference. Live every moment with passion.

2. Be grateful. If all you got was more of what you have, that is plenty.

3. Be kind. As Mother Teresa said, "There are only 3 important things in life: 1. Be kind. 2. Be kind. 3. Be kind.

4. Happiness is a choice. For every minute we are angry, we lose 60 seconds of happiness. Celebrate your happiness by never questioning it.

Alec's 5th birthday and Asher's first birthday party at Peter Piper Pizza

I'm going to miss being with them so much. Riding bikes. Fishing in the ponds at Chaparral park. Swimming lessons. Making rocket ships out of dishwasher boxes. DQ blizzards. Turning to him and saying, "You're my Pumpkin Spice" at Starbucks. Eating donut balls. Reading books in bed. Digging for bugs, dance parties listening to Michael Jackson, watching the movie Shrek over and over, snuggling with him and Cow Cow, constructing wooden train tracks all over the house, his smell, the feel of his orange- blondish hair. Our pillow fights, Alec bouncing on the bed and Asher trying best to keep up, double-fisted hot dog eating, seeing Ashie squeal for the blow dryer, hearing Alejandro say, "Laurie, put that baby down, he will never learn to walk and you are going to throw out your hip",

So here we are, my boys, me, us. I taught you about them so that when you think of Alec and Asher, you think of <u>them</u>. Do not give this senseless act of hate any credence. It is senseless to try to understand an inexplicable act of evil.

Alec and Asher came into the world against all odds. So many wonderful people were routing for them, for us. Many of you often referred to the boys as if they were their own. "How are my babies?" you'd ask. Alec and Asher were something of a collective victory. And now, eight hundred of us are mourning a communal loss. It's beyond missing the boys. Their giggles tinkle like crystal in our memory, where everything is jeweled. This is where they live now.

Thank you for loving us and thank you for loving me.

"I did it. I told them about my babies. I am so proud of them and of myself", I said to myself as I took my seat. But now what? Shiva? Sitting? There isn't anything in front of me, just pain, crying, condolences that bring no relief and a calendar, full of deleted events whose only purpose now is to track the death of my kids and how long I have been away from them. It is a black hole and I am sure that it is just a matter of time before I get sucked into it.

I want to go back.

I want Alec and Asher.

I want to go home...

Antarctica

"When going through hell, keep going".

-Steven Wiggs

THE FIRST TIME THAT ALEJANDRO picked up the girls after the boys died, he took Adele and Juliet to our neighborhood park to tell them what had happened. Now under no circumstance should a 6 year old and a 4 year old kid be told that a father, who is supposed to protect and guard his kids against danger, murdered them by shooting them in the head. No way. It is difficult enough for an adult brain to hear that and, comprehend it, if at all, there is no way a child can. And how would these babies sleep at night? What would the thought be, "If Daddy gets mad enough, he may shoot me? Or if my Mom and Dad are fighting, one of them will kill us to get back at the other?". No way, a little brain will not be able to digest this. Especially given the nature of Alejandro's relationship with his ex-wife which was less than amicable.

We decided to tell Adele and Juliet a reasonable scenario that these little babes could understand, at least for now. In time, we will tell them what happened, as it is part of their lives now too, but they will be told when they are able to comprehend it.

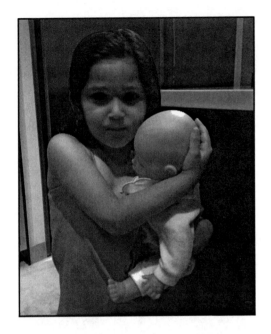

Juliet with her "Ashie" doll

Alejandro: "Adele, Juliet, I need to tell you something that happened to Alec and Ashie, they got hurt real bad with their Daddy". Alejandro explained.

Adele: "What happened Daddy? How did they get hurt?"

Alejandro: "They got into a car accident baby. Their body was so hurt that they couldn't get better, their heart tried to pump and pump, but it just couldn't".

Juliet: "Why didn't they take them to a hospital? They have doctors there like you that can make them better".

Alejandro: "They tried to baby but they were too hurt".

Adele: "Did their Dad die too?" asked Adele.

Alejandro: "No, he's alive but hurt really bad".

Juliet: "I'm going to miss them so much. I loved Ashie especially, he was my baby that I carried around. Now all I have is my big Ashie doll to carry around, he is the biggest of all my dolls.

Adele: "Did it hurt? To die?", she asked.

Alejandro: "No baby, they didn't feel a thing, they were sleeping when it happened".

When they arrived home, after greeting my extended family, they asked if they could go to their rooms, Adele just wanted to be alone on her bed and Juliet stomped up the stairs with a somber face and a huge announcement.

Juliet: "I need to go take care of Laurie, something very bad has happened to Alec and Ashie".

Colombia, May 2010

The girls are so incredibly sweet and delicate with me. One night, as I was sitting on the couch in my usual place, they asked me…" Laurie, would you like to stay here and live with us now that Alec and Ashie are in Heaven?". "I'd like that, thank you. I'd like that very much".

The next few months are a blur for me but one thing was for sure, there is such a thing as Groundhog Day. My routine was the same, every day; I would wake up, help get the girls ready for school, prepare the children's lunches (Alejandro has Adele and Juliet 50% of the time), make breakfast, kiss Alejandro good-bye and take the kids to school. Painful. I had to become really good at hiding my feelings and quick. Alejandro and the kids were watching me closely, they can see everything, and I wanted to make sure to protect them, as best I can against this beast called grief. Once I dropped them off, I would come home and lay in the casita bedroom where I carefully made the bed with Alec's bedspread. I chose the casita because it was away from the main house, further from the street, impossible to be interrupted just in case Alejandro would come home early or on the days that the housekeeper would come. I would lay there for hours, moaning from the bowels of my soul, like a wounded animal, slowly dying. Looking back, I like to describe it as having an adult tantrum, as if on some level, if I pushed back hard enough, loud enough, long enough, time would begin to turn backwards and I would get my kids back. I was so angry, I didn't want to dress his kids and feed his kids, I wanted mine, I wanted to care for my kids. Of course, this had nothing to do with Adele, Juliet or Alejandro, it only had to do with me and my rejection and argument with reality. I cared very much for Adele and Juliet, and of course Alejandro, these people invited me in.

"Oh my baby, what can I do for you?", asked Alejandro as he wiped my eyes.

I just looked at him, my God I wish that he could do something, but there is nothing to do. This is so frightening, when there are no more moves. This is it. I have died. On the inside. I will spend the rest of my life sitting, unable to move, unable to ever feel happy again. I will live wanting nothing but my kids, and anything that I do receive will feel second-best and will always return me to their death. Look at this sweet man, he would do anything for me. Little does he know that he is looking at a corpse. It is just a matter of time before he realizes that I am dead and there is nothing for me to offer him, no giggles, no singing, no passion, just a shell. He will grow tired of this, of me. Who wouldn't? Who would be able to withstand this? And for what? I know that we are crazy about each other and it has been an incredible 8 months but just like the boys, it will die soon. No one can survive this. Maybe a possible survivable situation would be one child, and of course under the circumstance of a natural cause, cancer, a car accident, SIDS, but not murder. Not two children. No way. And certainly no relationship could prevail from this wreckage. Eighty percent of all marriages end in divorce after the sudden death or severe handicap of a child, how could a dating couple do it? This is too much for me to handle, but then again, everything has been taken from me, so am I really going to feel the injury of another loss?

"Can you call Steve for me? Would you ask him to come over?".

Steve is, as I call him, my spiritual teacher. We met about six years ago, he was the Chief Legal Officer for Maricopa County mental health services and I was his clinical liaison to the mental health courts. That was one of the most amazing positions that I held. My role was to propose to the presiding judges' clinical recommendations and interventions for my "consumers" in lieu of incarceration, with the goal of rehabilitation and recovery. It was a very innovative concept, Maricopa County was one of the first in the country to lead this initiatives of mental health reform and I was in the thick of it. Most of the offenses were considered low level crimes of living such as theft, shoplifting, trespassing, or drug addiction. I remember one consumer, "Daisy", she was an African- American woman, however, according to genetics and anatomy, she was a he. What crime had she committed? Theft. She had stolen her mother's credit card to get breast implants and I was tasked with making clinical recommendations to the Commissioner Well, obviously, we cannot return the product stolen, I recommended therapy to help her responsibly process her gender transformation and of course, to repay the money back through employment. Month after month, Daisy would come into court, beautiful, long hair weaves, nails to perfection, a Von Dutch handbag and dressed to the nines. She looked fabulous but was not going to therapy and there was no repayment. I avowed to the judge that Daisy has stated that her position is that, "she did what she had to do to become a woman and that is not a crime". Therapy was not going to touch this, as this was Daisy's unwavering truth. In the last court proceeding, the judge issued a final warning to Daisy to comply with his order or she will be held responsible for her crime and the penalty by being remanded to serve jail time. Daisy came back a month later, no change, and the order issued. Jail. And in jail, they send you on the unit as dictated by your genitals, not by your orientation. There was never a dull moment in our court.

One would never suspect that behind this tall, Anglo-looking man is a practicing shaman-like truth-seeker. Steve's preceptors were don Miguel Ruiz, author of <u>The Four Agreements</u> and Barbara Emerys, they are Masters in transformational wisdom called Toltec Dreaming, a philosophy based on beliefs rooted back to the time of the Toltecs. The premise is that life is not real; we are all living a dream. We are in a program, being programmed about what things mean and how we are supposed to believe, feel, and act. It is a story about what you think is real about life that limits us, it is all a dream. Life is art and we all have the ability to create and design the life that we want. Steve and I would meet monthly to reflect on concepts of being and the symbolism of objects and concepts, from money, to our names, to death. Well, I need Steve now, because this is very real. This is not a dream. I am in hell and it is real.

"Laurie, baby, Steve's here", Alejandro said as he escorted him to me and gently gave me a kiss on my forehead.

"I'll be in the casita, let me know if I you need anything".

"Hi love, it's good to be with you".

"Hi".

We must have looked at each other for at least a minute, my eyes struggled to keep him in focus through my tears.

"What now? This is really real Steve, it's not a dream. They are dead. He killed them".

"That is true my love, he did. But we need to look at this. We need to look at his act and we need to find the truth of the boys and death".

I sat there, open, with baited breath, waiting on his every word, as if God was speaking through him, ready to give me the answer.

"Ego will use memory to get us to put our attention on the atrocity of the past, which is nothing more than the perennially, tired lie of our separation from love being replayed over and over.

The image of "lost bodies", of "death" is purposive, to hold us hostage to the dream of death and to keep us "out of our mind", believing that we too, are just a body so we choose not to wake up. The dream of death is a lie that the bodies could never contain the pure innocence of the power of love. There is no separation or death in reality, but only in illusions".

"Laurie, I want you to remember, the choice is whether we give our attention to the past story of separation, the story being, "since you can't see their bodies, they are gone" and remain hostage to ego's recipe for suffering, or whether we give our attention to the present reminder of truth of our mutual and indivisible innocence, an innocence which those beautiful, smiling images of Alec and Asher continue to reflect back to your mind".

"I got it. It's Easter, the symbol of resurrection, where the Master woke up from the dream of death and showed us that we too, could awaken. It had nothing to do with the body, but everything to do with a mind choosing Life".

I continued. "Alec and Asher are nothing more or less than images of Innocence (Spirit) beckoning me to come Home, gently calling me to awaken when I am ready. They, nor I, have their bodies any longer, but the lie was that if one is not embodied, then they disappear, they die, and that is simply not true".

"You got it angel", Steve said as he sat back with paternal pride.

"It hurts so bad though, the human in me wants to smell them, hold them, hear them".

"I know, but that is the body. The body wants to feel, hear, see, not Spirit. So we need to be gentle with this body, this adaptation that it will go through, and be patient with your mind, it is at war right now".

I don't know how we did it, but for a little while, I felt relief. Relief was possible, even if it was for 15 minutes. I was in horrible pain but I got a hiatus.

"All my love my beautiful sister" Steve said as I hugged him good bye. In my moment of relief, I decided to walk, it felt good to be outside, to be where they live, in the sunshine, to feel the wind that they also feel, that they are a part of. It is incredible how I forgot how good it felt to move, to walk, to witness that I am alive. I am sure that this is a foreign concept to many who have not encountered a physical or emotional trauma, but sometimes just getting up is an extraordinary accomplishment. Now that might be considered a miracle for an infant or young toddler, but for a forty-year old woman? Well, I say yes, it is. Being is painful, sitting is painful, horribly painful, and what makes it even more painful, is that you know it hurts to just lay or sit but it is more painful and takes an exorbitant effort to live, to move. This concept of inertia is powerful, a property of matter by which it continues in its existing state of rest or uniform motion in a straight line, unless that state is changed by an external force. External force? Like a bullet? I guess this did change my state. Is it possible that this new course is me, stuck? Unable to move? Unable to live? I am scared that hell is my new reality with no exit. Or worse, purgatory.

So here I am, my new home. Alejandro gave me free reign to redecorate the house, you know, "make it my own". He needed a new couch anyways, it was obvious how angry of a person his ex-wife was by the scarce articles that she left behind, a flat screen TV, a bed for the girls, their old mattress and an old couch. Redecorating was a nice distraction for me from my existence, painting walls, new furniture, but that was short lived. Somedays, in between my torturous crying sessions and furniture deliveries, I would wander to the office where I would look at pictures and videos of the boys. It was not painful at this time to look at their images, it made me feel close to them. But something began to happen, the images were becoming painful, I found more and more, that they did not bring me comfort, they just made me long for the boys more. This is horrible, so now I can't even find comfort in my boys' pictures? Ronnie and William, my best friends would come over every day and check on me, I would leave the front door open so they could let themselves in. Sometimes we would just sit, sometimes I miraculously would have the energy to make a sandwich. I hate sandwiches. Maybe that is the litmus test for how much I cared, or didn't. They would always offer if I wanted to go for a walk or out to lunch just to the corner, but I would always refuse. I wasn't going out there, too much effort, too many people, too representative of a world that is going on without me. I had no desire nor energy to fake it, smile at a waiter or listen to people talk at the table next to me about what they are doing over the summer vacation.

I can say that I picked the best, best friends. They really are not my best friends, I consider myself, as they do as well, family. William, Ronnie and I met about five years before, William was a Medical Director of Children and Family services and I was one of his clinical directors. He was prim and proper, so conservative, a good southern boy, reserved in his mannerisms, but I saw right though that. The ice was broken quickly when I put a post it with the writing," How deep was it?" next to his Vanderbilt Medical School class picture where he sported a huge 1979 afro. Not bad for a white guy. Behind closed doors, it was all glitter between us.

Ronnie on the other hand was flamboyant, feathers and fabulous in every step, or should I say, sachet. They have been together as partners for 28 years, I was the daughter they always wanted but never had due to obvious anatomical circumstances.

I spent the next six months thinking about how I am going to go back "out there", in the real world, to this aborted life that I hated and was filled with destruction. My supervisor was getting heat from the Administration to post my job, as my disability was coming to an end and Alejandro knew that the longer I stayed out of work, the harder it would be to go back. I remember feeling outraged by both, the very thought of asking me to go back to work, to life, it felt so insensitive and callous, but I knew that they were right.

The first day back at work was brutal. I was only going to return part time for now and my supervisor was agreeable for me just working as long as I could. Oh God, how am I going to do this, the looks, the comments, the whispers behind my back? "I can do this. No I can't", I thought to myself.

'Wait. I need to stop", I said as I walked towards the cardiac unit. "I can't".

It's like there is an invisible force stopping me.

"Take your time Laurie. No rush.", my supervisor said.

I am having a panic attack, I have never had one before. My heart is going a mile a minute, I am paralyzed, I can't move.

"OK, let's do this". I said.

You are OK, nothing is going to happen to you, all we need to do is make it to your chair. Then we are going to get your census. Then we are going to turn on the computer...you can do this Laurie. I hear Alec, "It's OK Mom, it's OK". I was just like a kid on the first day of kindergarten, terrified to leave her mother. And look at me, I am getting comfort from the words of my 5 year old son.

Every day that I entered work became easier and easier, people were amazingly sensitive but it is a mixed bag at how people show up. Grief and death are so taboo in our society, especially trauma and sudden death of a child. No one really knows what to say or how and when to say it, and say what? I'm so sorry? That was a beautiful service? I know that they are in Heaven looking down on us? I believe that people are so amazingly kind and sensitive, but I also know, as do they, that there is not a goddamn thing that could be said or offered to bring comfort. Nothing. So I had to get really good at this and set the scene, for them and for me. Whenever people would give me the look or start to cry when they look at me, I would just say," I know, thank you, I know. Now let's focus on what we are doing right now". I also know that if someone did not say anything, it meant nothing other than that, there was nothing to offer. But just because there was an absence of discussion or overt grief, it didn't mean they didn't care or have feelings about it. I am sure, no different than myself, that many people have a lot of anger. What are they supposed to do, emotionally vomit all over me and tell me what a repulsive animal, stupid asshole my ex-husband is? Or that we should kill him without a trial? No one was exempt from the wave of grief caused on March 31, 2010. No one.

Andre had been brought to my hospital's sister campus, it was also Alejandro's hospital. All of Alejandro's colleagues were up in arms, no one wanted to treat him, not the intensivists, not the

ICU nurses, not the case managers. No one. Everyone was appalled. The Administration managed to get a clinical team to treat him, he was under police arrest 24/7 in the ICU, not only for our protection but for his as well. It turns out that Andre botched his suicide attempt after he killed the boys. He put the gun in his mouth and pulled the trigger, but apparently, he flinched. The gun moved and blew a bullet out his cheek. His brain and the rest of his face were unscathed. Instead of trying again, he called 911 and told them of his deadly act. Plan B. Suicide by cop. But that failed too. He chickened out. He apparently had posted a sign on the front door saying, "DO NOT ENTER, CALL 911". All he had to do when the SWAT team busted in the door was to move, just make one sudden move and they would have blasted him. But fear got the best of him. I am still not sure whether that is fortunate or not. For him, for me, for us.

Andre was in stable condition, he was on a vent to assist his breathing because he shot part of his tongue off as well, so there was a lot of tissue trauma and the physicians wanted to make sure that they protected his airway. Other than that, he was intact, he had a brain that was working and was 100 % fully aware of what he had done and his present circumstances. Now that is an additional definition of hell.

I will never forget the day, I had just gotten off of work and arrived home for lunch and my afternoon sleeping session, usually either 3 hours before I have to pick Adele and Juliet up from school or for 5 hours before Alejandro arrived home on his off-parenting time days. I opened up my email and there it was, in my INBOX, an email from Andre. I froze. He's out? He's free?

To: Laurie

From: Andre

Re: Louis

I'm sure you aren't doing well. How's Louis doing?

Andre

Oh my God, How's Louis? Louis (nickname for Louis Vuitton) is our Siamese cat that he got me as a gift for my 32nd birthday. How's Louis? You murder my two children and you have the nerve to inquire about my cat? What a sick son of a bitch. I ran to lock the door and grabbed the phone to call my attorney Randall Udelman. I had been taken in like a stray by Randy a day after the boys were killed, his daughters went to Temple Solel preschool and knew that I would need representation and assistance in navigating the trial years ahead as a victim.

"Randy, he's out! Andre is out! He's free!", I screamed hysterically.

"What, slow down, what happened?". Randy gasped.

"I just got an email from him, how could he be free? How could he be emailing   me?"

"Hold on, send me the email. But first of all, where are you?", he asked.

"I'm at home, at Alejandro's. All of the doors are locked, but he knows where Alejandro lives".

"Give me one minute".

That minute seemed like an eternity. I ran outside and hid behind a tree. If he were to come to the house, I would not be trapped, he would not see me and if he did, I would make a scene. There is no way he is going to kill me.

"Laurie, OK, I just called the hospital, he is there, he is in the ICU under arrest, there is a policeman at the door 24/7".

Relief.

"How did he send this? How does he have access to a computer?".

"It turns out that the nurse forgot to log off of the computer in his room after she finished charting. I have spoken with the police, Detective Lockerby and the ICU Nurse Manager, this will not happen again. I am so sorry. You are safe. He is not free and will never be free again."

What a psychopath, he has no conscience. How about caring about your children? Or a murder? Sick.

That was it, sheer terror that he was free. And what if he was able to be free? What if they found him not guilty? Then what? I would have to run away. My kids would have been murdered and he would get off Scott free? And what is the point of my life, ordering oxygen and placing patients into rehab facilities? It's too much. I am being tortured, from the inside and the outside, when I am awake and when I am asleep.

I can't do this anymore. I can't live here, this place is no longer habitable. And everyone would understand. I just need to hold on long enough for the trial, then I am complete. I have made my decision, if he goes to jail, I'm done, if he is set free, I'm done.

I now know where I am going and that is unstoppable and undeniable, but how did I get *here*?

PART TWO

PATH OF THE PAST

The Color Pink,
the Color Blue

Clinging to anything makes us unhappy.

June, 1996:

"It's so hard to date, the profiles, the censored first impressions, the expectations…what if I just wanted someone to go feed the ducks with?", I remember saying to him. That was the start, "If you ever want to go feed the ducks, I'd like that". I thought to myself, " Gosh, this guy is kind, gentle, witty", it seemed so effortless. Yes, we came from different backgrounds, I was Jewish, he was a recovering Catholic (as he referred to himself), my parents were married 40 years at the time, he was a latch key kid, left by his father at age 3 and a victim of physical and emotional abuse by an alcoholic step father and a codependent mother. But none of that mattered to me, maybe that is the "pro-underdog" social worker spirit worker in me who just believes in people, not about where they grew up, how much money they had or what their parents did for a living. I found my life partner. I had just finished my Masters in Social Work with a specialization in chemical dependency and trauma and was now setting my eyes on my personal life. Andre and I were married after an effortless two year courtship on April 26, 1998. Life was good, we were like two baby squirrels who were on their own, playing, exploring the world and gathering our nuts for the future, a baby, a house, retirement. Our careers were on the fast track, I was promoted to a director position of overseeing 23 mental health clinics in Maricopa County and Andre achieved the #1 position for sales in the United States for Breitling watch sales. Just like two birds gathering sticks, yarn, and branches of the sort to prepare their nest for a baby bird, so were we.

It was August, 2000 and we had been trying to conceive for about 18 months. My Dad, who is an OBGYN, made some suggestions but my body was not hearing it. After 2 miscarriages and 2 tubal pregnancies, 4 visits to the emergency room to get methotrexate injections (an injection that aborts any further growth of fetal cells so my fallopian tubes would not rupture from a tubal pregnancy or have bleeding complications), we moved to try artificial insemination. Bingo! We got pregnant on the first try. I know this will work, I told them at the doctor's office, just put the baby in me, I'll take care of the rest. I loved being pregnant, some women dread it or complain about the tender breasts, morning sickness or clothes that no longer fit, but not me, I relished in it. My first OB appointment was thrilling, and not only was I going to have a baby, but I was pregnant with twins! I had released 2 eggs and Andre's boys saw fit to have their way. I have always been a petite girl, how I was going to carry 2 babies was beyond me, but I knew my own grit. We were beyond ecstatic, my belly was growing exponentially every week, I didn't care; I was going to be a mom.

I was referred to a hematologist/oncologist, Dr. Sharon Ondreyco, to monitor my blood levels, to make sure that my immune system would not attack these fast growing fetal cells. She was amazing, we called her "song bird" because when she speaks, it is as if she is carrying a tune." Helllllo Laaaaaurie, it sooooo great to seeee you. How are the baaaaabies today?". I loved seeing her and exchanging pregnancy stories, you see we had a common bond, she was a mother of twins as well. Weeks and months went by and Dr. Ondreyco was diligently monitoring my blood; she was especially interested in particular white blood cells called eosinophils. Eosinophils are tasked to fight off infection or foreign bodies and since the body sometimes does not distinguish between certain fast growing cells, we needed to make sure my body wasn't mistaking fetal cells (which are fast growing and rapidly dividing cells) with other foreign, rapidly multiplying cells (cancer, parasites, infection). My levels looked amazing, HCG continued to rise, WBC remained down. I was under surveillance for about 6 months and all remained quiet inside, my belly was huge and I was loving every minute of it. We were home free.

I'll never forget that feeling. It was a Saturday morning like any other. Andre went to work and I was cat napping around the house with my 24 week pregnant belly. I loved those days where I would play music for them by putting earphones on my belly, sit in my rocking chair and dream of what color I would paint their room, it was heaven to me, a dream that was coming true. Poof. There it was, a drop. Not a drop of liquid, but a drop inside, like an elevator that was suspended all of the sudden was giving way. I called my OB's office and of course, told me to go to St. Joseph's Hospital. There? Why? It's not my hospital that I am going to deliver at, it's so far away. I drove myself there and parked my car in the short term visitor's lot. " I'll just be a few hours, no big deal. Gosh, I love this car", I thought as I grabbed my purse from the backseat, catching an eye of 2 vacant car seats. It's a symbol of a family to come, it would be filled with happy times; looking in my rear view mirror as my twin babes sing Britney Spears songs together, Cheerios scattered on the seats and a make-shift changing table in the back. I was escorted to the OB emergency area and upon exam, I knew that I was not leaving soon. "Your sac is coming out". As the daughter of an OBGYN, I knew too much. As a girl, I loved accompanying my father to the hospital, back in those days before the time of law suits, birthing bathtubs and HIPAA, we were allowed to go into the delivery room, unlike now where there are restrictions on the restrictions. I must have seen over 20 babies being born. After I was wheeled off to a room and quickly put into the Trendelenburg position (legs elevated so gravity will assist the body), I called Andre, then my parents. Strangely, I feel confident that this is just a glitch, Dad was on his was, he wouldn't let anything happen, not on his watch, not with a baby. Unfortunately, not fast enough...the airlines only offered one direct flight a day from Miami, FL to Phoenix so they were routed through Charlotte, NC but they were coming. A few hours later, the on call obstetrician came in accompanied by a fresh class of medical students and residents, looking at me as if I were a specimen in a lab. "We have to do an amniocentesis to see if the amniotic sac is ruptured. What we will do is inject blue dye into the sac, if it leaks out blue amniotic fluid, it will confirm that the sac is open and bacteria will inevitably and quickly seep in, if it is, we know that the babies will be compromised". Compromised? What the f**k does that mean? I hate that term. it's so nebulous, so politically correct for transmitting medical messages. It could mean anything from the babies having developmental delays and growth challenges to being dead. No matter what they proposed, it didn't matter, stick a 13 inch needle in my stomach, I would do anything to save the babies. I laid there for another 24 hours, seeming like an eternity. The doctors pumped me up with Magnesium sulfate, a lovely IV cocktail that lessens contractions but makes you have double vision and feel woozy. "Go home", I said to Andre, "I am just here baking the babies. I am fine, you need rest". So there I was, just me and my twin girls. Tomorrow, the needle, the future revealed. As I laid there, I noticed a crucifix of Jesus on the wall, after all, this was a Catholic hospital. Even though I was born Jewish and had been practicing Buddhism for years, I looked at the cross and said a prayer. " I know that you are from God, please watch over my girls, guide us to a safe place". With that, I closed my eyes and let myself dream of my twins, my girls, my family to be.

" Laurie, I need you to wake up, I'm Dr. Crandall, I am a perinatologist. I need to talk to you about the babies". It was dark in the room, he sat down in a chair, somewhat casually and sighed. " What time is it? Are they OK?", I said as I looked blurry-eyed at the fetal monitor. It was 2:30am. He then started on his monologue, one that I am sure he has said far too many times to hopeful mothers to be. "Tomorrow we will find out the integrity of the amniotic sac but you need to know that if the babies need to be delivered, we most likely cannot save them at 24 weeks. If they do survive, they most likely will be blind, deaf and have severe disabilities such as an inability to walk, cerebral palsy, liver and kidney problems". I understood what was being said to me but I was unable to comprehend this death sentence. " We need to discuss first what is going on with your body, your kidneys are also taking a toll in trying to keep the babies, you are becoming sick yourself". Sick? Once again, I didn't care, I just wanted to keep the babies. "What are you saying? What does sick mean?'. "Your kidneys are becoming stressed out and as a result, there is a lot of blood and protein in your urine, we don't want you to go into acute kidney failure". "Are there any questions that you have for me?". "No, I need to think about this and talk to my Dad and husband". He left, as quickly as he entered, the transaction was over, as if he was delivering a pizza. So the decision has shifted? This wasn't what was proposed to me yesterday? I don't want a new plan, I want our old plan; you would stick a needle in me, the sac would be intact, I would lay here for 6 more weeks and then the babies can come out. Now it was a decision between my life and theirs? If I choose them, I die and possibly them too. If they do live, they will be horribly disabled and I know that Andre would not be able to care for them, and on top of that, I may be on dialysis or need a kidney transplant. If I choose my life, then I am giving up on them. How does a mother even conceive of making that decision? I can't give up on them, but it is a dead end, regardless of my choice, they will not get to live. Incompatible with life. That's the term. But what do we do if this situation, this decision is incompatible with my life? With what I want? It's not fair. But then again, what is this concept of fairness I thought to myself as I laid there. Question: "Why my babies? Why me?". Answer: "Well whose babies should die? Why not you? I am posing my demands and disposition on this place, what I want, not what it offers, and if I don't get what I want, then somehow it is unfair, cruel, withholding. It's not that this place doesn't care, it's just that it doesn't function like that. I learned that years ago from my work of Byron Katie. What a God send she is. Now I see what she meant. I have never wanted to escape my body more than I did at that moment. There was nothing left to do. I didn't have the choice of being on strict bedrest until the babies can be sustained in the NIC-U. I am trapped. Andre came in that morning and I told him the news that the grim reaper shared. " Let's just see what the amniocentesis shows, maybe he was wrong". He was such a great cheerleader, always looking for the positive. The amniocentesis was just as the grim reaper expected, blue, there it was. I don't care for that color blue to this day, for it holds a story of my fatal circumstances; bacteria, sepsis, death. The choice had been made for me, I needed to let them go. But it wouldn't be that easy...

"That is not an option here", the nurse said. "I don't understand, the doctors confirmed that it is my life or theirs, they can't make it out here and I will not survive myself to bring them to the point. What do you mean it's not an option?" I replied. "Here, this is a Catholic hospital, all lives are equal in the eyes of God. We will not interfere with the choice of who lives or dies first". "But I am Jewish!", I was screaming from the inside, on the outside, I just looked as if someone was speaking Swahili to me. "We will need to transport you to another hospital if that is your position." "My position? It is not a poker game or a political debate, this is my life!". Once again, the line was moved. I was glad to be transferred, it is a sad commentary but the only way that I can relate to how I am feeling right now is similar to a person in Austria in 1933, being asked if they would like to leave. I was transferred to a neighboring hospital, alone at 3:30am, of course when all transfers happen, in the middle of the night. I was wheeled into the OB unit, past the nursing station where I glanced at the patient board: "Laurie L: 24w 3d. I saw the rest of the mothers to be: Jan B: 29w 5d, Susan R: 31w 3d, Katie D: 30w 2d. God what I would give to have their numbers, their babies have a chance.

Me, I get to swallow a small pill in about an hour that will cause my amniotic sac to spontaneously rupture and the babies will slip out. They each would be about a pound, no labor, no pushing, just a giant eruption. Just then, my Mom and Dad came in. He's here, my Dad is here, he will make it OK. "Talk to them Dad, see if there is any way to save them. I don't want to let them go, I don't want to do this". He looked at me with tears in his eyes and said," I know, but there is nothing to do and I don't want to lose my baby". So that's it, there were no more moves left. Checkmate. After I settled in and all of the patient assessment checkboxes were complete, a nurse by the name of Socorro came in, I'll never forget that name, the name "Socorro" in Spanish means "to help or relief". It meant none of that to me unless she could save my babies. She was going to have the honors of giving me the poison pill, for the babies, for my dream. I felt so guilty. What did I do to cause the sac to drop? What could I have done to have prevented this? How could I choose my life? How could I not choose my life? I'm so angry, everyone else gets to have a normal pregnancy, why not me? Socorro handed me the pill, I held it for about 2 minutes, it felt like an eternity. She didn't go anywhere, she just stood there, staring at me. Why was she witnessing me? Why? Did she think I wouldn't? Can't I just wait? I took it. It's over. I closed my eyes and wept until I cried myself to sleep. Maybe if I sleep, I will wake up and I will realize that this is all just a nightmare.

"HELP! GET SOCORRO," I screamed to Andre. "Where's my Dad?!". "He went downstairs, he will be right back, it's OK, just hold on". "Marcia (my Mom), get Jason back here", Andre commanded. There was a gushing explosion that I felt in between my legs. It worked, the poison was effortlessly taking my babies away from me, those girls that I tirelessly tried to have for 2 years, were slipping away, literally. I closed my eyes because I didn't want to see them, I couldn't. I didn't want my last memory of them to be this. I wanted to remember them in me, feeling them swirl around in my belly, seeing them on the ultrasound snuggling with each other. I felt them though, I felt a leg against my thigh, I couldn't wait until you came and I could touch you, but not this way. Not this way. That was all I remember.

"Where's Laurie?", my Dad asked Andre, weeping in the corner as he entered the dark room. "They took her away, she started to bleed, they couldn't stop it, she's in the operating room". Suddenly a nurse frantically appeared, "Andre, we need you, come with me quickly, you have to be with her". I could not imagine what my parents were feeling, or could I. My babies were slipping away and so was theirs. An unstoppable train racing down the tracks with a cliff straight ahead.

I woke up with a white light, it felt so warm and peaceful, I was not scared. "Get me more blood!", I heard, but I didn't care, I was not there, I was witnessing the doctors and could see myself down there, but I was not there, I was above. "Keep her here, talk to her, Now! You have to make sure she stays connected to you. Just keep talking to her". I heard Andre's voice, it was comforting but I was already so comfortable, it was effortless to be, to exist. I only knew what had happened afterwards when the family debriefing occurred. It turns out that because I was only 24 weeks along, the vessels and placenta are let's just say, really rigid". These huge vessels that are sustaining a placenta and 2 lives while symbiotically existing off of another is not ready to be shut down. In a 40 week, normal full-term pregnancy, your body prepares itself to separate. At 24 weeks, not a chance. The uterus was not bearing down so I was bleeding out. I had lost 2 pints of blood and a third pint was in my future. I was in shock, so the spirit leaves, it has its own journey, is preparing to be separated from the body. Some call it a NDE (near death experience), or an out of body experience, for me, it was the inseverable, intertwined spirit of a mother, who would never leave her kids.

"Laurie? Laurie?.,". It was Andre. "Where am I?". I was shivering, my body was surrounded by plastic air bladders all over my body, this device was tasked with raising my core body temperature. I guess that's what happens when you lose 3 pints, you freeze. I didn't know what had happened but I knew that I was here, not there. It didn't feel peaceful, my spirit was reattached to this body and I knew that the dream had ended. I was no longer pregnant. I was a mother but my babies were dead. No nursery, no Babies R Us, no playdates. I am so disappointed. I knew that I had chosen my physical life but how could I live in this body without them, with this story. This story is incompatible with life. The following day a social worker came in to offer me some pamphlets on grief and support groups. "I am a social worker too, I don't need any pamphlets, thank you". Pamphlets? Support groups? What could someone possibly say or scribe in a leaflet to make me feel better, to fill this hole, to provide some relief from my dream that was bored from my soul? I want to go home, get me out of here. Not so fast. If losing my children was not sufficient, there was more. "Where would you like for us to take the children? What are your last wishes for their remains?". I have to bury them? A funeral? No, I can't do this, I have been tortured enough. According to Arizona law, any fetus over 16 weeks is considered a person and must have his/her remains put to rest appropriately. I can't do this. Ok, I can do this. I am their Mom, it is my privilege and responsibility, my honor to lay them to rest. I chose a beautiful cemetery , one that had an area for babies and children. I couldn't go there, not yet, I just knew where I wanted them to be. Andre took care of the details with my Dad. Later that day, with nothing left to do, I put on my old pregnancy clothes (that was painful) and was wheeled to the front entrance, where Andre would escort me home, yes, in my SUV, the vehicle that we bought to tote our girls around now it felt like a hearse. He couldn't retrieve the car fast enough, as I waited at the entrance of the hospital in my wheelchair, I looked to my left, a mother holding her baby, to the right, a mother holding her baby. I was in hell. Me, I had a bag that said," Patient belongings" and a plastic hospital tray in case I threw up in the car.

I came in the house, there was no celebration banner with "Congratulations" written on it, no cribs in their room, just silence. "Are they buried?", I whispered. "Yes, they are alright, they are next to a boy who was 4 years old. He will watch over them. Let's just sit". We must have sat side by side for hours, it felt like days. In silence. In disbelief. So now what? Go back to work? Go out to try a new restaurant? I didn't want any of that; the future was a blank for me. Everything had been erased, like God had held down the "delete" button too long and had erased my story. "Take down the cribs and return them to Babies R Us, and close their bedroom door". The door to the girls' room was a portal that transported me to the past, to hell with no exit.

I spent the next 6 months licking my wounds, I didn't have a great deal of interest to socialize, what is there to talk about? Not having kids? How the babies died? When we will try again? My friends were so amazing, they would just visit with me and sit, just witness me in my space. They knew me, they knew that there was nothing to say, just unstoppable tears and then we would look at each other after a while and say, "Ok, so I need to get some waterproof mascara". That would make us laugh because there was really nothing to say that could help, just a moment of frivolous comic relief to validate and mark the magnitude of what just happened. I had to return to work, that sucked. For anyone who has experienced grief, you know that it leaves you with the feeling that anything that you were doing before the loss, seems so insignificant and pointless. Everything you do is slower, harder and more painful. I looked really pretty on the outside but on the inside, it was ugly. Every morning was like preparing to go on stage, "Costume and make up please, 15 minutes before curtain call!", that's what it felt like. Sometimes I guess we have to fake it until we make it. But make it to what? What I wanted has vanished. Yes, I am helping people but my spirit is stuck in the past. My most important job was to guard and carry those babies. I failed. So what if I am a great clinician or meet my deliverables on an action plan? Nothing is as important as the job that I had to involuntarily resigned from. So here was the choice in front of me, dream another dream or don't.

The choice was mine, to be happy or to suffer.

THE BEAST INSIDE

Sometimes it is in the darkest skies that we see the brightest stars.

- Juliet Morales

JULY, 2001

I made it. I was alive and so was the insatiable desire to be a Mom. Andre and I were back on our baby making path, I had licked my wounds from the loss of the twins and we were determined that this time would be different. We tried a few more times with no success, not surprising. So here we go again. We found a great reproductive endocrinologist, Dr. Moffitt. We knew the routine, the horse-sized testosterone pellets that I would need to inject in my butt, the freaky mood swings from the high level of hormones, the multiple weekly, trans-vaginal ultrasounds to measure egg follicle size, and worse of all, the anticipation of that little plus or negative sign on the end of a dipstick. Any woman who has been through infertility knows exactly what I am talking about, it is all consuming but in the end, it will all be worth it. This time was different though, I was feeling a bit off, maybe it was the medicines, maybe it was the residual anxiety from the trauma, work stress or maybe it's just all in my head.

I had been promoted to Director of Utilization Review in Maricopa Country for the country's largest private managed care company and loving it. When I was not sitting in Dr. Moffitt's waiting room, I was tasked to advocate for approximately 14,000 seriously mentally ill clients in 23 mental health clinics across Maricopa County, educating and guiding clinical teams. My focus was early intervention in the hopes of preventing psychiatric relapses that would lead to prolonged, disruptive hospital stays and to ensure that once a client was ready for discharge they had all of the resources necessary to facilitate wellness at home. After the death of my girls, in my own way, I related to my clients. They didn't ask to have a mental illness, be it schizophrenia, bipolar disorder, major depression or any of the like. One day they were living their lives, and in the next moment, they were different, their reality was surreal: hearing voices, having erratic mood swings and even found themselves involuntarily petitioned to be hospitalized against their will. Mental illness had taken their dreams, whatever that may be. A doctor. A mother. A place to call home. Or how about just the ability to sit in peace and read a book. Just like I didn't ask for an incompetent cervix, I got it and they got their condition to battle. I now understood how it feels to take that poison pill, a medicine that you know will incapacitate you by blurring your vision, affecting your organs, makes you nauseous and tethers you to a bed. You just want to feel better but the path to healing is unbearable at times. Even those who don't want the treatment find that their personal power and dignity of individual choice is taken, you find yourself with a nurse in front of you, monitoring you to ensure that you took that pill. When and how did we find ourselves being treated as less trustworthy or deserving of a voice? I now got it, that term *empowerment* that we throw around casually in clinical meetings or social policy classrooms. It is not something that we give to the patient, it is something that they find within and give to themselves, our role is to simply support it. If a person is able, capable and willing, the decision does not belong to us as healthcare workers, it belongs to the person who is faced with and has to live with the decision. Hospital admissions should never be casual decisions, regardless, they never were for me. But now than ever before, did I understand how important it was for me to educate clinicians and capture how to promote the power of patient choice. I no longer needed to imagine what it feels like to be confined to a hospital where decisions were being made for me, around me, with poor to no options available to bring relief. There is no escaping one's body or brain, I know that all too well.

We flew home to Miami that summer, it felt good to return home, play and be reunited with my parents outside of a hospital and enjoy the life that I fought so valiantly to have. "How was your flight?", my Dad asked. "Good, you know, uneventful, but I want you to feel this", I said to my Dad as I placed his hands around my neck. My Dad had always said that I have the longest neck, like Audrey Hepburn. "Do you see the vessels bulging out? I feel like my head is going to explode sometimes". "I see what you are talking about, a lot of times these symptoms are related to hormone levels, let's get some blood work and a Doppler ultrasound scan of your neck and see what is going on". Throughout the vacation, the symptoms were on and off, it felt as if I was doing a handstand and the blood was rushing to my face. I redirected my brain, interpreting the symptoms as due to the hormones. To me, this small discomfort is exactly that, I'll endure this if it ensures that my body will be ready to carry a baby.

I returned to Phoenix and scheduled the ultrasound, I thought it was a waste of time, my blood pressure was normal, my labs were normal, what could they possibly find? It was a Friday, I left the hospital early for the imaging center, once again, parking my car in the short-term visitors' parking lot. The ultrasound technician began slathering the petroleum jelly in my neck, I let my mind wander, dreaming away of my next ultrasound, the *good* kind of ultrasound that I will hopefully have soon, the one that will reveal a baby. "Excuse me for a minute Laurie, I'll be right back". "That's strange", I thought to myself, but then again, maybe not, people are stretched so thin in today's world, multi-tasking. The technician soon returned with a radiologist who took over. Now being the daughter of a physician, I knew what this meant, whatever she had stumbled upon, she entered into deep waters, she found herself in a place where she was over her head and needed to call in the "big guns". It felt like I was waiting an eternity in purgatory as he moved the ultrasound wand around my neck and upper chest area. It sounds so petty but at times, I thought to myself that this is all unnecessary, he is getting petroleum jelly all over me and I have a date with my honey after this. "What do you see? What are you looking at?". The lights came on, "Laurie, we need to admit you to the hospital. Your jugular vein is 90% occluded and you are at a very high risk for having a stroke, we need you to go immediately to the hospital, I don't want you to go home, call your husband and have him meet you there". I will never forget my response, it shows just how surreal this was to me. "But I have a 4:00pm appointment to get my hair done, I have plans tonight to go to a concert with my honey". I called Andre, then my Dad. God dammit. Again. Are you kidding me, again? A stroke? Burying my children isn't enough, near death isn't enough? There's a chance that I will be dead? Or worse than death for me, trapped inside this body, unable to move or speak? He has to be mistaken, I am only 30 years old, I am healthy, I just rode my bike 30 miles? I walked down the hall, like that convicted prisoner John Coffey in the movie, <u>Green Mile.</u> I could hear the whispers, *"Dead man walking"*. Get in the car Laurie, just get in the car and drive. I sat there for about 10 minutes, should I leave? Should I just go home? The doctor said no, no going home. Dangerous. What if I stroke out while I am driving? I don't want to go to the hospital, I don't want to be a patient. I have to go, whatever this physician saw, I needed to have it checked out. Dammit, I hate this. I drove myself to the hospital, Andre quickly in tow and my parents already packing their bags for another emergency flight to Phoenix. I knew the routine, nursing assessments, check boxes, but this time it was different, why were they taking me to the oncology floor? Who knows, maybe they ran out of medical/surgical beds. Being a hospital administrator, I know the game of "bed juggling" improvisation of resources. *"I* was OK, *I'm* not like the rest of them", I reassured myself as I passed by other patients' rooms, heading towards mine, peeping in as we all do, rubber-necking to see what that person looks like, only to serve as a reaffirmation of what we don't want for ourselves and to convince ourselves that *our* condition is not as bad. Andre had arrived at the hospital followed by my best friends William and Ronnie. They really are not my best friends, I consider myself, as they do as well, their daughter. William, Ronnie and I met about five years before, William was a Medical Director of Children and Family services and I was one of his clinical directors. He was prim and proper, so conservative, a "good southern boy", reserved in his mannerisms, but I saw right though that. The ice was broken quickly when

I put a post it with the writing," How deep was it?" next to his Vanderbilt Medical School class picture where he sported a huge 1979 afro. Not bad for a white guy. Behind closed doors, it was all glitter between us. Ronnie on the other hand was flamboyant, feathers and fabulous in every step, or should I say, sachet. They have been together as partners for 28 years, I was the daughter they always wanted but never had due to obvious anatomical circumstances. "Gosh Laurie, you are *so* high maintenance, if you wanted some attention, you could have just asked us to take you out to dinner or to braid your hair!". We laughed. We had to find some humor and levity in this moment or else it seemed that we would all be sucked under by the invisible whirlpool of a story that was lurking in the back of all of our minds. Stroke. Paralysis. Unable to speak. Dead at 30. The nurse came in and asked me to change into a hospital gown and to remind me to try to relax, lay down and remain as still as possible because they do not know the integrity of the clot. Allow me to decode this medical instruction: *"Chill out, this thing can break loose at any moment and be sent to your lungs, where by you will consciously suffocate and die (or not), either way, it's big trouble and the shit is going to hit the fan"*. Got it, thank you; I am clear on the intensity of the situation. I obediently changed into the starched, snapped up hospital gown, protective not to show my backside to the world, and carefully got into bed. "That color just eats you up alive darling, do you think we can request a different color", exclaimed Ronnie. "I agree", William chimed in, "and this lighting is horrible, it just washes you out and that has nothing to do with your jugular vein". I just love how they care for me, they see me, they know what I need and what I don't. One would never know that they are brilliant, ivy league educated physicians if we were caught in an eavesdropping moment. It got quiet for a minute, I turned and looked at them with tears in my eyes and said," I want you to get me an Advanced Directive form". They looked at me with supportive, loving eyes and knew we had to have this conversation. "I do not want to be trapped *in here,* please know this. If I am in a coma or paralyzed without an ability to ever move again or talk to you, please, do not do anything. Let me go. And just know, that if you don't and I am staring at you, unable to speak or move and you want to know what I am thinking, here it is...I AM SO PISSED THAT YOU DIDN'T LISTEN TO ME TO LET ME GO!". We cried and just held each other. They all got it, everyone was on board. No matter what the next moment would unfold, my directive was clear.

I went for my MRI, my first one ever. That was fun, "so this is what a coffin feels like, I am in a coffin", I panicked. "Get me out of here", I screamed, I began to panic. "Let's give her some Ativan to sedate her", I heard the tech tell the nurse. "No, that is not necessary. Can you just give me a minute to collect myself, just slow it down for a minute?" I had to be aware of what was happening to me, I had to remain in control. "Ok Laurie, let's get a grip. This is what we will do. Just like when you were delivering the twins...Close your eyes. When your eyes are closed, it's less scary. Just let your imagination see what you want to see. When they slide you into the tube, if you can't see anything, then we can be anywhere". That's just what I did, 45 minutes and hundreds of buzzes, alerts, clanging sounds and clicks later, it was over, I made it. I returned to my room to find my family. My Mom and Dad just arrived, of course recovering from their own panic because it was deja vu for them as well. Hospital room, no Laurie, silence. I bursted into tears when I returned to my room and saw that they were here. "I am so sorry". " Hi honey, I'm glad we are here together. You know, if you wanted us to come, you didn't have to go through all of this", we laughed and just hugged each other. I was starving, hours went by, still no results. There was nothing left to do but wait and of course, like any self- respecting Jewish family, we ordered Chinese food.

Enter stage left, Nurse Scott entered my room, "We need to start an IV and give you a shot in your stomach, it's called Lovenox, it will start to dissolve the clot". In my stomach? "How big is the needle?!". It turned out to be a short needle that subcutaneously is injected into one's fat layer, not a big deal, just pick an inch, that is if I had some fat to cushion the stick. Phew, that's over. Hours went by and we realized that no physician was going to be visiting, it was late and we all were exhausted. Before my family left, I huddled them close, one last time, to review my directives. Don't intervene if the clot breaks loose. We gave kisses and they left," Don't worry, I'll be here in the morning, bring me a bagel because you know that the hospital food won't be a match for my picky self". With that, the door closed and I was left alone. Just me. I laid back in bed but my wandering, undistracted brain was dangerous. I turned on the television until I fell asleep. It was 2:30 a.m. and I was thrust out of sleep by a thought, "Oh my God, I know what happened, I know why I have this mass. It was the blood transfusions, I must have contracted something from the 3 pints of blood that I had received from delivering the twins. Oh my God, do I have HIV? Or some funky blood disease? Can you get cancer from a transfusion? My mind was wild, it was demanding to find out answers. I felt contaminated, how did I infect myself? What am I infected with? Did I borrow more trouble when I was trying to save my own life? Who knows, I guess the answers will be revealed to me, in time, tomorrow. I must try and get some sleep, impossible in a hospital and really impossible now with this story swirling in my brain.

My family arrived around 7:00 a.m., being a family of physicians, we know that rounds start early and we needed everyone to be front and center when the playbook is revealed. A physician accompanied by 6 other proteges entered shortly after, "Here it comes so brace yourself," I thought to myself. After introductions and bantering back and forth with my father about the practice of medicine and the state of healthcare, he redirected his focus to this ticking time bomb nestled in the center of my chest. " We need to take a biopsy of the mass that is sitting behind your heart, it's actually located in the center of your chest area called the mediastinum." "What's that?", I asked. "The mediastinum is the space in the chest that contains all the chest organs except the lungs, you know, the heart, the aorta, the thymus gland, the chest portion of the trachea, the esophagus, and some important nerves". OK, T.M.I., that's all I have to say. My "lizard brain", which I refer to as that primal, primitive voice that doesn't have an edit button, is now freaking out. "So, you'll have to cut my chest open? How do you get around my heart?". I'm going to have a gigantic scar right down the middle of my chest as a reminder of how my body betrayed me or did I betray it?

"No, no, we will insert a needle through your chest, guided by a CT scan and take a small sample of the mass, you will not require surgery to do this, it is a simple procedure". Thirteen-inch needle, through my chest, past my heart, and I am conscious? This does not sound simple. After Dr. Hoarsley left with his herd of residents like cattle that just finished grazing, there we were, the clock was ticking until the procedure at 2:00 p.m. and the time bomb was inside of me. I want to go home. I felt like a trapped animal, I was caged inside of this situation, this body, this hospital bed.

Not a chance, they came shortly after to wheel me downstairs, I asked my Dad to go with me, I knew that I needed his brain to watch over what was about to occur, I needed his centering. Everyone referred to my Dad for years as "Buddha", his disposition is similar to the willow tree that bends, he is like the stork, patiently waiting for what appears in the still pond, he is like the condor that flies above and sees what others cannot see. He stayed with me until they escorted him to the observation room, a small monitoring room that overlooks the procedure room. He signaled to me in our way, he pointed to his chest, then to his eye, then to me. "I see you". It was our code, we witness each other, we would not let each other go.

Pop! I will never forget that feeling, it was a violent puncture that I felt in my chest wall as they entered, "don't move Laurie, you are doing good", coached the nurse. "Come on baby, close your eyes", I tell myself, it's too late, I can't. I just looked around, I looked at her with begging eyes, as to help me escape. I couldn't see anything but blue: blue hairnets, sterile draping, blue masks. I hate that color blue. The only thing that I could control was my focus. I concentrated on my chest, going up and down, feeling the air being transported in and out of my nostrils, my logic was simple, if I was breathing, then I am alive. However, many minutes later, the procedure was over. I am not sure if they got what they needed, but it was complete. The Lovenox was dissolving the clot nicely, but so was I, sinking into a psychological abyss. Fear, anxiety and depression. I needed to get out of here, I was a flower that was slowly wilting. I don't know how they did it, maybe if you have enough physicians in your family, the rules are bent, but I was issued a pass to leave the hospital grounds for 4 hours. It was like a prisoner being granted furrow status. Where did I want to go, I didn't care, just anywhere. Guess where we ended up? You got it, the mall. I am confident that I was the only patron walking around the mall with an IV (locked of course). It felt so good to be among the living, not the sick, the waiting or the dying. I tried to buy something but nothing attracted me, I remember thinking to myself just how down I really was if I was unenthused by my favorite stores.

I was discharged home the following day where I tried to get some grip of planning my week, but I was in purgatory, that is until tomorrow when I find out the biopsy results. God, please don't let me have HIV or some funky blood disorder, please tell me it is nothing, let me be the one case where I stump the doctors and they stand in front of me baffled, but "free to go".

I went to my PCP's office to retrieve the news and get my "plan"; either I was going to be set free or I was in ither it was going to be smooth sailing or dire straits, either way, the path would be revealed. Now mind you, I've never met this physician before, why would I, I have never needed a PCP, I was a healthy 30-year-old woman and if I ever did need something, I could just ask my Dad or William. Here it comes… "Laurie, the biopsy results came back and I am sorry to have to tell you that you have cancer." Cancer. The "C" word. "You're dead". That's what any-one who has been told these 3 words really hears. "You have Hod-gkin's Lymphoma", she continued. She droned on and on about how this is "one of the best cancers to have and that it is very curable". I didn't hear anything else that followed that sentence. She sounded like Charlie Brown's teacher to me at that point," Mwaaahh, mwaahh, mwahh". I put my head in my hands and just wept, I'm going to die. I just got handed a death sentence, here's our hourglass. I will never forget this thought for as long as I live, "God, if you are trying to kill me, it is working. But why are you killing me slowly, consciously?". God dammit, I chose the wrong door, I should have let myself die, I chose *my* life instead of the girls, and for what, so I could die a slow, painful death 6 months later? I felt so much anger. And somehow, her best pep talk was to encourage me to feel grateful that I was stricken with a "good cancer"? F-you! How about that. How about no cancer, that's the best kind to have?!

OK, time out, let me give you the low down, Hodgkin's 101... This is a rare beast, predominantly found in males between the ages of 15-35 years old (except for the rare nodular sclerosis variation), one usually does not know that they have it until it has spread like wildfire, you know, Stage 4 and metastatic. It's an insidious cancer, one of the triplets from the blood cancer family, as I refer to them as; leukemia, lymphoma, myeloma. You know, the cancers that roam around your body, swirling in every crevasse, exposing every organ and cell to the malignancy, conquering areas like the Crusades of Europe. The annual incidence of Hodgkin's lymphoma is 2.7 per 100,000 per persons per year and it had to find me? Then again, let's ask the question, "who should it find? Why not me?". Oh yeah, I know, I found the answer to this question in the last hospital admission. The lymphatic system is part of our circulatory system that fights against infection and immunizes us, comprised of the liver, bone marrow, lymph nodes and spleen, Hodgkin's has free reign of your entire body, anywhere your circulatory system goes. Our immune system has particular infection fighting cells called B cells that are found in my lymph nodes. What happens is that these B cells develop a mutation in its DNA, the mutation tells the cells to divide rapidly and to continue living when a healthy cell would die. The mutation causes a large number of oversized, abnormal B cells to accumulate in the lymphatic system, where they crowd out healthy cells and cause the signs and symptoms of Hodgkin's lymphoma. Stage 1A is the best, no symptoms, the cancer is limited to one lymph node or one organ, above the diaphragm. Stage 4B: in several areas, above and below the diaphragm, in bones, organs and lungs. Let's just say you're f**ked.

I had no signs or symptoms to alarm me that a coup was occurring within me. Night sweats? No. Unexplained weight loss? No. Itching? No. Fever and chills? No. Persistent fatigue? Well, Yes, but now let's look at this…I just lost 2 babies, had 3 blood transfusions, almost lost my life and am jacked up on more testosterone that a body builder so OK, maybe a little fatigue, but who the hell would have thought of cancer? But how did I get it? This type of cancer is so rare? Was I correct, did I contract this from the blood transfusions? Was it caused by my dabbling with stimulants in my freshman year of college? Was it from eating Oreos? How did we miss it? Dr. Ondreyco was monitoring me like a hawk, we were watching my immune system like crazy, if there was a hint of cancer, we would have detected it in my weekly CBC. It was lurking in the shadows this entire time, waiting, multiplying.

Dr. Grateful wasn't done yet, there was more… "Laurie, we need you to have another surgery, not to treat it but we need to get more tissue to confirm that it is Hodgkin's, you see, there wasn't enough tissue obtained from the needle biopsy. Once we are sure, you will need to be staged, meaning how extensive has the cancer progressed." "Let me get this straight, you want me to go back to the hospital?". I was a freed bird that was being put back in the cage.

The next few days were a blur, I feverishly scoured the internet, looking on any and every website I could find to understand this beast that lives inside of me. I learned that Dr. Grateful was correct. I was lucky, if you can call it luck, to have Hodgkin's lymphoma, it is a very treatable cancer, even considered curable, but I would have to go through hell to reclaim my life back. Surgery, staging, chemo, radiation, possibly bone marrow transplant.

Please let me have Stage 1A, please, please. Pleading with God about cancer is so surreal and somewhat comical when you think about it, it is such an insane mind game. We banter back and forth with this Oneness, knowing in our sane mind that it doesn't work like that. It's not that God doesn't care, it's just that this place and He, (whoever you believe or don't believe in), simply does not function in our framework of bargaining and contingencies, we all can relate to it, Christmas is a classic example. A child is asked if they have behaved either naughty or nice, then asks Santa Clause to complete their wish list, if they get the gift that they want, Santa is a hero, if not, he is a malignant, uncaring tyrant. It is my observation, that this is how we as humans posture when we approach God a great deal of the time, regardless of what we are asking for. If we receive what we want, He is a loving Father, if not, he is a punishing King who is ignoring and not listening. The line keeps being moved, but we continue to chase it in the hopes that we will be the one who gets saved. It sounds like this:

"Please don't let me have cancer, I'll do anything that you ask."

"OK, fine, I have cancer, but let it be a good kind of cancer"

"So, I have this type of cancer, please let it be localized and not metastatic"

"I'm not doing chemotherapy, I am only willing to have radiation"

"OK, I'll do chemo but I don't want the kind that makes me lose my hair"

"Check mate, I have to have chemo and radiation, but this is the first and last time that I am going to do this"

"It's back, I'll try again".

Staging sucked, the surgery, the PET scan, the bone marrow biopsy. Andre was amazing through the entire process; he was my rock, my cheerleader, my silver lining. I remember when I was getting the bone marrow biopsy, a lovely procedure where the doctor makes a small incision in the area of your spine near your butt, then inserts a hollow needle through the bone and into the bone marrow. Using a syringe attached to the needle, the doctor withdraws a sample of the liquid portion of the bone marrow and then graduates to a larger needle to withdraw a sample of solid bone marrow tissue. Imaging a hollowed corkscrew, that's what it felt like. I was so scared, just as I began to cry, Andre turned around with two tongue depressors in his mouth like a chipmunk and said in helium-pitched voice," Don't cry my love, it will be over soon, it's just you and me here". I just busted up laughing, he knew exactly what I needed to prevent me from having a nervous breakdown.

I now appreciated the power of a procedure. In the medical world, we say that no procedure is benign, thinking along the lines of physical risk for injury, secondary infection or recovery.

But I am talking about the emotional risks and invisible trauma that goes unspoken. In this current day in age of lawyers, malpractice suits and physician review boards, physicians all too often order tests to, let's say, C.Y.A. (cover your ass) and patients are all too eager to demand and pressure the clinicians to perform an unnecessary battery of tests. Believe me, I want to know what is going on in me and to have an accurate diagnosis, however, we as patients have a greater responsibility, greater than the health-care workers that we hire to treat us, to protect ourselves, not just physically but most of all, psychologically. More tests are not always better for us, every time we are scanned, prodded, told to tell our story, every time that a needle is inserted into our vein or cut on, it is traumatic, not just to our body but to our spirit. We have to mentally prepare for what is about to happen, asking ourselves not *if* it will hurt but how badly will it hurt, we are looked at but not seen, we are surveyed, assessed and categorized. It is going into battle, there is no way else to say it. We are mounting a defense in preparation to win a war against an invisible enemy that can ambush you at any moment, and you become weaker and weaker as the days go by. The ambush may come before, the waiting, the anticipation, during the procedure or afterwards while sitting on pins and needles as the results are read. It takes energy to prepare, strategize, deploy and recover from any battle, a fight is a fight, and make no mistakes, there is trauma in every offensive or defensive move.

I was cut at my neck, as if someone had slit my throat. A surgery that was supposed to take 45 minutes lasted 3 1/2 hours. Apparently the cancer had presented like a sheet of Saran wrap around my neck and chest area. Dr. Toporoff, the surgeon (great bedside manner by the way) kept fishing for bits and pieces of tissue. He would pause in his scavenger hunt to collect more tissue as the samples were rushed to the pathology lab only to receive the response, "Inconclusive, we need more". They were looking for these elusive B cells called Reed-Sternberg cells that are found in my lymph nodes. Finally, no stone was left unturned. I had bone marrow extracted, PET scans that made my lymph nodes light up like a Christmas tree and the long awaited appearance from the cellular stars of the show, the presence of Reed-Sternberg cells, we had a diagnosis: Hodgkin's Lymphoma, nodular sclerosis variation. Funny, I never was so happy to have a diagnosis.

Now I understand what they were thinking on my first admission to the hospital when I was admitted to the oncology floor, it wasn't because they didn't have any medical/surgical beds. They had a hunch: 30-year-old active female, sudden unexplained head pressure, jugular vein 90% occluded, mass in medial sternum = Preliminary diagnosis: cancer. They nailed it. As I was wheeled down the hallway upon discharging from the hospital, I passed the chemotherapy treatment rooms: large sterile rooms lined on the periphery with Lay Z Boy recliners and accompanied IV poles. I saw *them*, the people whose club I was now an involuntary member of, pale, sullen, sickly and of course, bald. There were my options that lay ahead of me: be proud of your baldness (hopefully one will have a nice, shaped head), live however many days or months of life ahead wearing a cap, hat or scarf or even worse, wearing a really bad wig. "I am not doing this, f**k that, I'll fight cancer but I refuse to look like that", I adamantly declared to Andre. He just looked at me with supportive, empathetic eyes but we both knew that I wasn't calling the shots on this one. I was dropped into an unwanted reality, again, Austria, 1933. No escape.

This can't be happening, it was all too surreal. What the hell happened? This was like deja vu but the bad kind. I was sitting in Songbird's waiting room, this time it was me that was seeing the holy grail for a cure; I wasn't a mother, I wasn't pregnant, I was one of *them*. This was a cruel joke, I mean come on, if God had a sense of humor, this was not funny. Or maybe it wasn't about irony, maybe the "greater" purpose of meeting Songbird wasn't for the twins; He knew that there was a secondary reason. After hugs and tears from all of the girls in the front office, I was called back to my usual exam room, but this walk back was different, it was as if I was walking towards a cliff, ready to either be pushed or jump, either way, it was painful, slower, harder. I used to bounce in down these halls effervescently, the bubbles in champagne, now I was flat soda.

Songbird entered my exam room, but this time, she was not singing, the song was abruptly deafened by cancer. "I've been thinking a lot about what happened and I think I know how we got here". She had the answer to one of my biggest questions. I anxiously leaned forward, almost falling off the end of the table, as if she held the direct word from God. "Without getting into too many clinical details, I'll explain this to you. When some-one becomes pregnant, our body automatically defaults to an im-mune-suppressed state in order to protect the rapidly growing fetal cells from being attacked by the body itself. Because your immune system was suppressed, not only on its own but also from the medicines, our treatment interventions not only allowed those beautiful girls to develop but unfortunately, it also facilitat-ed the Hodgkin's Lymphoma cells to multiply." "So, if it wasn't for my pregnancy with the girls, I would have never known that I had cancer until it was too late?", I asked. "Correct, Hodgkin's

Lymphoma a lot of the time flies below the radar, sometimes even undetectable for years, by the time the symptoms are experienced, it's considerably advanced." OK God, so truth is revealed, you are not a cruel ruler with a malignant sense of humor (no pun intended), the twins were a gift, but I could never have planned it to be packaged this way and it certainly didn't feel like one. Indirectly and directly, the spiritual intention of the girls' lives was never to be fulfilled here, their sole (and soul) purpose was to come into being so that my life would be saved. I believed, just like all of us do, regardless of culture, race, ethnicity or species, that it is the mother that makes the sacrifice for her children, even if it means compromising her own life, but that is not how it works. On the contrary, it was the babies who had given their lives for me, they were the protectors. I had been given my life back, twice. I couldn't hide from this, it was like trying to escape sunlight. My life and spirit had a greater purpose, my body was spared, I got the good kind of cancer, I got the earliest stage, I got Songbird. There is a Master plan that had a Higher Being's fingerprints all over it and it was organically unfolding right in front of my eyes. Once again, here I was, standing at a crossroads, on the other side of a miracle. But once again, I would have to fight to get my life back.

Let's Go To War

"You can't stop the waves but you can learn to surf"
- Joseph Goldstein

AUGUST, 2001:
"OK, here we go, deep breath Mom and Dad, you want to see what I look like with blonde hair?", as I held their hands standing at the entrance to the wig shop. I just look at them with a big smile as if it could protect us all from breaking out in tears. "I have a 10:00 appointment with Gabrielle", I said as I looked around at all of the wigs on the mannequins. "Welcome, I'm Gabrielle. Wow, you have beautiful hair". "Thank you, I'd love to donate it to *Locks of Love* but it's already falling out in clumps, it'll never make it". Gabrielle escorted us to a private fitting room and disappeared to retrieve some wigs that has some resemblance to my natural hair. Andre was so upset that he couldn't be here for me, I know that he has to work so he can take as many days off as he could for when I needed him the most, on my chemo days. My Dad kissed me on the top of my head and gave me that *look* as he tried to hide another huge clump of hair appearing in his hand, but there was no concealing the fall-out from the chemo. "I am so sorry Laurie, this is just one of the saddest days of my life",

as his eyes welled up. I grabbed his face, "Daddy, it's OK, I'm going to be alright". I didn't believe it, but I had to do something to comfort his fear. He is witnessing his daughter slipping away from him, again, and there was not a damn thing that he could do about it. My Mom tries to be a rock but she just sat there and swallowed her tears. I know this place, I'm the one who has lost children, not you. Let me be the strong one, give me your pain and fear in exchange for the confidence to let you know that I am not afraid.

People have asked if I am going to a support group, but for me, no way. It's not that I have anything against support groups, for heaven's sake, I'm a therapist. It's just a timing, thing. It's like going to a hugging group when you don't want to be touched. I didn't want to relate to those people. It was my only defense that I had at the time to reject cancer, to give it a big F you, to say, "I want nothing of you to identify me by". I don't know if it would help but right now, I don't want or need anyone to relate to, I don't want it to be a part of me, in any way, physically, psychologically, spiritually, not now. I am going to sequester it from seeping into my identity. It may not be what others choose, but it works for me, I need to protect my personal power, my life force, and by keeping it as "outside" of me as far as I can, allows me to do so.

"I must say, I look pretty good, it's doesn't look or feel as bad as I thought it would". Don't get me wrong, I won't miss the day that I no longer have to wear it, but for me, it was better than looking like my diagnosis. I want to wear my cancer on the inside of me. " When we get done with this, I am going to throw a huge party, a "Celebration of Life" party" I exclaimed, "We have a lot to celebrate. It will be a faux pas party". "Why a faux pas party?", my Mom asked. "Because cancer creates faux pas, it causes me to look, act or show up in ways that I would never imagine. You know, like when I sat in the Lay Z Boy display in the middle of Costco for 20 minutes because I was so fatigued but told everyone that I was a furniture model? And I don't care how great a wig, scarf or hat is, when you don't have any eyebrows or eyelashes, your make up and face just throws the entire look off. I have to admit, cancer does benefit me in a way, in addition to birthing tumors, it also gives rise to an attitude of irreverence to etiquette, when you are fighting for your life and feel like crap all of the time, you realize that either life is too short to impress others or that it simply takes too much energy", I remarked. As I looked at myself in the mirror, I straightened my wig and said, "Ok, let's do this".

Chemotherapy is so barbaric, it is unbelievable that this is the best thing that modern medicine has to offer. Some of these chemicals are so toxic, that the chemotherapy nurse giving the drugs is suited up in a "bunny suit", similar to a Hazmat suit that the scientists wore in the movie E.T. when they were treating the alien. It is so ironic, as for the recipient, no protection offered, just shoot it into our veins and let the magic happen. Chemo is an equal opportunity murderer, killing the good cells that are tasked to run this body as it should and keeping me alive while hopefully attacking the bad, those that threaten to steal the grains of sand from my invisible hourglass. I knew that I would have to reframe this experience, the hair loss, the bone pain, the fatigue, the mouth sores, I could not sink down the rabbit hole again for months; living in the story of a disempowered victim, looking at my body as if it was a traitor, a vessel that has failed me and then a victim itself, trampled on by the war that was just waged on it.

I'll never forget where I was that day, that moment will be forever inscribed on my brain for as long as I live along with some of the other sentinel events that I hold close to me: when President Reagan was shot, the explosion of the Challenger, the death of my grandmothers, the day I found out that I was pregnant, again, the day I knew that I wasn't, again. September 11, 2001, I was identical to every other citizen of the world when they heard the news. I can recall exactly where I was, what I was doing, what I was thinking as I watched helplessly. Paralyzed with disbelief. I was standing in my kitchen, watching the footage of the first plane when it hit the North tower, then the South. I saw people jumping out of the buildings, trying to escape, what a choice, jump or be burned to death. On a very basic, human level, I could relate to them. I too was under attack by a terrorist, however my terrorist was different though, it was living inside of me, stealth upon arrival, uncaring and indifferent to my life. My salvation, on the other hand, would arrive tomorrow at 8:00 a.m. in the form of IV tubing, deadly upon impact but also uncaring to the casualties of this war. I was given a chance to live, my hero would have the opportunity to reach me. The next day was a blur, it seemed as if I was hanging out, waiting to see the results of the attack by Al-Qaeda, waiting for strategy, waiting for a war on all fronts. Would the U.S. be OK? Would I be OK? What does the future hold?

Chemo #1, Day 1: This is D-Day. I stood in front of my mirror, my hair held tightly in high pig tails, my beautiful hair that would soon collect on my pillow. I wore a pink and white shirt that said, "I make boys cry". For the next 5 minutes or so, I began to kick box, jabbing, kicking, hooking left, then right as I looked at myself, pumping my spirit up, talking to myself, "Bring it on mother f**ker because you picked the wrong body to be in. This is war and I am taking back what is mine, it's my body to live in". With that, I was ready.

The phone rang, I heard Andre talking, it was Songbird's office. "OK, I will tell her, please let us know as soon as you can". "What's going on?", I said. "As you know, all planes are grounded. And our chemo is on one of those planes. "What? I can't get chemo? How long will I have to wait? All of the sudden, I felt desperate, horribly desperate, like a clock was ticking, the bomb was ready to detonate and the lights went off right before I could diffuse it. No chemo. As I sat down and slowly disassembled my pig tails, I sat and cried for them, for me, for us. I was indirectly being murdered by those hateful, terrorist bastards, I guess cancer comes in all forms, ours was called Al- Qaeda. The ripple effects of terrorism are sometimes delayed, subtle, trickling down to the small nooks and crannies of lives, places that cannot be seen and that are not reported in a news article. What a f**king nightmare, my country was at war, thousands of people were murdered in front of our eyes, I am being slowly destroyed in front of my eyes, have a cure but it's inaccessible, to anyone, by anyone.

So, I sit, waiting. Waiting for the dust to settle, waiting for plane travel to resume, waiting for my poison, waiting to live, waiting to die. But waiting is painful, it may feel inert, lacking energy and action, but its process is slow, painful, destructive. When we wait for something, anything, anyone, it is a trick, our minds have set the stage for us to demand something, in our time, in our way, and we believe that once we have this, or don't have it, that we will be OK, happy, safe. I am powerless. Here's a thought...What if I didn't wait, what if I just went on with my life, go to work, eat the foods that I want, go where I want to go? What if I didn't wait for the world to give me what I wanted in my timeframe, but when it gives it to me, when it is offered? That certainly is less stressful. I like that, my job is to call Songbird's office every day to check on the chemo status and their job is to get the drugs. They know that I need it, I trust in them that they will advocate for me and that feels more peaceful than placing my timeline on the world. Either way, worrying and waiting or not, it wasn't going to make the chemotherapy appear sooner, it certainly wasn't going to help my mental condition and if anything, it might even harm me. It's clear then, I will not wait. I will not wait for something to save me, nor will I wait for something to kill me. This is called living.

Three days pass. Let's try this again. Pigtails? Check. Gallon of water? Check. Attitude? Check. As Scott Beemer said three short days ago," Let's roll".

The chemo routine looks like this: Day 1: Chemotherapy for 6 hours, sitting in a Laz Z Boy staring at others around you, your identical cancer twin, IV poles, no hair, sullen faces, counting down the time, drip by drip, wishing it would "hurry up" as life inside is being extinguished, one cell at a time. Our relationship with time is interesting, sometimes we want it to speed by, to go fast so we can get to the next event or to end a painful one. But then, there are moments where we wish time would stop, freeze or reverse, go back, unwind, so we can stay here, in this moment. Before the twins slipped out. Before cancer invaded. Day 2-5: the feeling of near death, extreme bone pain that could only be remedied by hot baths every hour, mouth ulcers that make my gums bleed and prevent me from eating, which makes me look even more like a concentration camp survivor, and extreme fatigue and weakness due to the obvious cellular destruction going on and loss of red blood cells. Andre was so amazing, the first chemo session, we were both terrified, what was going to happen? How was I going to feel? would I end up in the hospital because it would blow out my immune system? He ran to every health food store to retrieve "special" Vitamin C to support my immune system and sat vigil over me as I laid in bed, left with what seemed to be only breath and a heartbeat. And he is so sensitive, this sweet man wakes up every morning before I wake to clean away the newly fallen locks of hair off of my pillow so I won't have to witness it. I have such an amazing support system, when Andre travels, my Mom flies in and when she leaves, my girlfriends are the third wave in our reserve army of angels to care for me. I'll never forget the time when I called my friend Lindy who lives across the street from me to bring me a sandwich, she of course obliged and asked where I would like it from. I responded, "From my refrigerator". Now that's fatigue. Narcotics are out of the question for me, chemotherapy is already too constipating as a result of "good" cells being killed in my GI tract, plus I have no intention of beating cancer only to wrestle addiction. Day 6: I start to join the living, I will have a week off and then start all over again on Day 15. Six rounds, that's all I have to last in the ring for, well, until the next phase, radiation.

On the days where I was feeling better, I was insistent on returning to work, even if it was on a fragmented, part time schedule. The Chief Medical Officer is my boss and *the* boss, what he says, goes. If I was up to working, I could work, no need to take time off, no need to worry about short and long term disability, he just supports me in being where I could be and doing as much as I can. What a mensch. Work was a harbor from the storm and he knew it. It is a place of positive energy, advocacy, and strength, a place where I had purpose as a person, not a patient. It is engaging and stimulating to contribute to other people's lives and served as a respite where I could be involved in everything and anything other than cancer. Sometimes my friends and family apologize when they talk about their lives or other things other than my cancer, but for me, it is a welcomed relief. No apologies needed or wanted. If I could teach people who are supporting a person going through cancer, or any traumatic experience just one lesson, that would be to create a pocket of peace by talking about their lives, their struggles or reclaim that "normal" interaction as you had with them before the diagnosis or "that moment", talk about anything other than the elephant that sat down right in the middle of the room. It not only serves as a shelter but also reminds us that we are still ourselves, a person with interests, not a disease or a shell of a person with only a unilateral focus. It helps us take back control of our identity. I am Laurie, the same Laurie that likes talking about current events, politics and what new movies are coming out, being a "foody", discussing books with my book club, visiting furniture stores and open houses to see latest decor trends, listening to music, singing karaoke, and telling jokes. Cancer takes so much, don't worry, it won't be ignored, it *will* be talked about, there's no getting around it. But it is so important to remember to not let it take all of you, don't let it take everything.

"We made it", I screamed as I left Songbird's office, "No more chemo!". This torture was over, at least this kind. Who knows what radiation will feel like but from what I've read and have been told, it will basically just feel like an incredibly bad sunburn x 10 and will make you feel tired. Songbird says that the side effects from chemo therapy are not compounded but I don't believe it, I am living it. It's as if someone punches you in the eye, it begins to heal only to have it punched again in 2 weeks and then every 2 weeks after that for 3 months. There is no way it isn't compounded.

Now radiation is an interesting weapon on many levels. For those of you who haven't had the pleasure walking into a radiation room, the entrance door is about 2 feet thick, sort of like walking into a bank vault. It serves one purpose, to make sure nothing gets out or in. Yup, and this is what is going to be beamed into my flesh, no 3-foot door to protect me, just me, cancer and a laser beam. That's the first layer, the next has to do with sheer modesty. Since cancer decided to make a home in the center of my chest, it requires me to lie here, naked from the waist up with healthcare workers (yes, all males) and remain completely still as they map out the radiation points as if they were generals planning their invasion and I was the map. Why couldn't the cancer have been in my arm or head? I guess cancer is an equal opportunity invader, it doesn't care about my modesty or morals, it just shows up and conquers. This is one aspect of cancer that isn't shared on the radiation web site, irradiation of any sense of privacy or physical modesty. My girls were hanging out there for the world to see. I'm sure that they didn't care, it was no different for them than as if they were to be looking at someone's eye.

After the plotting, comes the mesh mask, it serves to pin down my head to the metal table so my head is completely still so when the radiation is released, it pin points the beam to the centimeter, one move or twitch and we are destroying healthy tissue, particular to me, critical vessels that are servicing my heart and lungs.

The months of radiation remind me of my days as a girl growing up in Miami, circa 1976. My weekends were spent with my grandparents at their condo on Miami Beach, building sand castles, jumping in the waves, and searching for shells from the dredged beaches. How does this relate to radiation as a 32-year-old woman? Easily, just 3 words; second degree burns. I walked around for the next eight weeks without a shirt, as much as I could, just like when I was a girl and stayed out in the sun too long. I looked like the poster child for promoting Coppertone sunscreen, the "before" picture of course.

Once again, deja vu. We left Songbird's office, like a prisoner being released from prison after serving their sentence. Don't look back. We are out of here, for at least 3 months anyways. It's so silly when I think about it, as if the nurse is going to come running out of the oncology office, waving lab results, screaming, "Wait, Laurie, there's been a mistake, you still have cancer. Come back!".

Our celebration of life party was a smash, anyone and everyone came who wanted to help us put a period at the end of this episode, and end to this fight to get my life back. Brown belts with black shoes, gold chains with charm holders, polyester jumpsuits, plaid shirt with horizontal striped skirts. It was all there. William and Ronnie were the judges, draped in rainbow boas of course and the DJ played our tribute song, "I Will Survive" by Gloria Gaynor. I did it. We did it. I crossed the finish line with my entire team of lovers with me to celebrate our milestone. I was officially in remission. Just a detour, that's all this was, now let's get back to my dream...to be a Mom.

THE COLOR ORANGE

*There is only one way to happiness and that is to
cease worrying about things that are beyond the
power of our will.*

- Epictetus

THE PATH TO ALEC was not an easy one. Three early miscarriages, IVF, the devastating loss of twin girls in the sixth
month of pregnancy, my diagnosis of and treatment for cancer.
And, finally, a return to our mission of having a family.

My body had made it quite clear it was not going to be in the
baby-making business, so we considered our options. I felt too
impatient at this stage, after all we had been through, to pursue
adoption. It was my mother who first brought up the idea of surrogacy. She suggested we think of it as a gift from my grandparents, who had left my generation of grandchildren a nice nest egg
and for whom nothing was more important than family.

As it happened, we began to center on the idea of surrogacy
right when Good Morning America's Joan Lunden was on the
cover of *People* magazine with her surrogate-born twins. It felt
like kismet. When things fail to go as planned, you look for signs
everywhere. Even on the cover of People magazine.

Andre surprised me with two plane tickets to California for an appointment at the Center for Surrogate Parenting in Burbank. Fourteen months, scores of interviews, dozens of medical, legal and psychological screenings, and tens of thousands of dollars later, our surrogate mother Traci, a thirty-eight-year-old mother of three, was pregnant. The doctors warned about the many possible complications, and Traci told them, "You just do your thing. I'll take care of the baby."

Which she did beautifully. Every month, I would fly out to Albuquerque where Traci lived, we would spend hours on her couch, side by side watching The Food Network, her gently guiding my hand to her growing abdomen when Alec moved; we were an amazing team. An unsaid language, an inexplicable bond.

Until the baby decided he wanted out, delivery date be damned. The call— "Traci's in labor, come to the hospital"—came weeks too early. As someone who has had several miscarriages and as the daughter of an OB/GYN, I knew what it meant to go into labor at thirty-three weeks. The baby wasn't finished baking yet, especially that intricate brain and those gossamer lungs. We rushed to the airport for the eternal forty-eight-minute shuttle to Albuquerque. When we landed, it was my cell phone voice mail that delivered the biggest news of my life: Traci had an emergency C-section. She is safe, the baby is safe. Come meet your son.

Alec Matthew: born December 8, 2004, at 10:04 a.m. I had always loved the name Alec, it means "protector of mankind", and Matthew is my Father's middle name, I wanted Alec to always have a little piece of my Daddy with him, his Papa. When we first arrived at the hospital, we went to see Traci first, after all, she was the bearer of life who helped bring our son to us, then on to the

NIC-U to meet our long-awaited miracle boy. "You ready?", Traci said, " I have been waiting every day since I had met you to give you your baby". We all wheeled down to the NIC-U with giddy anticipation. I squealed as softly as I could in a NIC-U, if that is even possible, as I looked on at a beautiful, brown haired boy, so small and pink in the huge open incubator. "No Laurie, that's

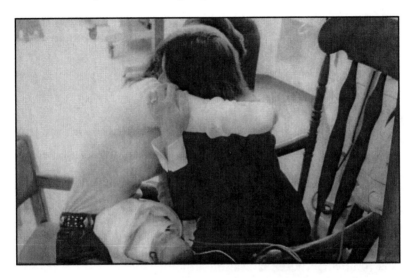

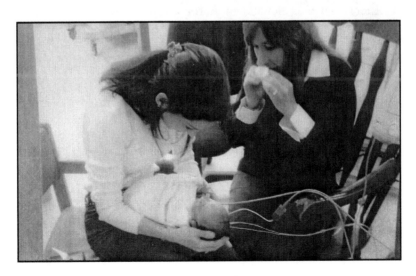

not Alec, that's Alec", Traci said pointing to this red-headed baby. "A Gingy, I got a Gingy?!", I said with elation. He was healthy, if tiny. The nurse handed Alec to me, but I refused, Traci and I knew had rehearsed this moment hundreds of times; they would hand Alec to Traci, then she would hand him to me, as it was her gift to give. I could hold him in his entirety in my two cupped hands. He had a beautiful head of golden red hair, which I took as an auspicious sign. In Israel, a redhead, a Gingy, is thought to be endowed by God with a special spirit. Alec certainly was.

He had a team fighting for him in that NICU, including, to my great surprise and delight, a neonatologist colleague of my father's from Miami who had traveled to Albuquerque for a month-long rotation. My parents, of course, quick to arrive, took turns bantering back and forth on who Alec would look like as they scrubbed up to enter the NIC-U when my Dad looked up to a calling of his name. "Jason, is that you?". "Andy? I don't believe it". Andy had arrived, I was convinced, to protect my Alec. At that moment, Andre made a soft announcement. "Laurie, Happy Mother's Day", as he put an Aaron Basha baby shoe inscribed with Alec's name around my neck. We all just hugged each other, we did it, I am a Mommy, and my baby is *here*, not there, here. Once again, my best thinking could not have planned Alec's birth this way, the happenings unfolding were simply too much to deny this master orchestration.

His fierce will—also part of that Gingy spirit—was evident from the moment he insisted on coming out weeks early. He was supposed to be fed from an NG tube (nasogastric, for those lucky enough to not know), but how he hated it. Although he weighed a little over four pounds and had lived on this earth for all of three days, he figured out how to get his way, pulling the tube free and thrashing against the nurse as she tried to reposition it. Finally, she conceded: Alec, 1; NG tube 0. When Andy came in and asked, "Why doesn't this baby have an NG tube?" the nurse responded matter-of-factly, "He doesn't want it. He's made his position quite clear." Indeed, he was ready to start sucking, swallowing and breathing all on his own.

Andre had to go back to work two days after the birth but returned two days later, driving eight hours nonstop through the desert to be with his new son. Andre was a natural-born father. He was as mesmerized as I was by this tiny creature with translucent skin and bright red hair. Andre was studious about parenthood. He paid more attention than I did when the nurses taught us how to put the palm-sized diaper on our preemie. He would be my teacher once we got home, helping me get the diapers facing the right way, not too loose, not too tight.

Sixteen days later, we took our baby home. Yes, on Christmas Eve. Now I am not a Christian but this is the best Christmas present ever. Our baby grew and thrived. His bright ginger hair stopped people on the street. But don't try telling him it was red. It seems that as soon as he could speak he took issue with the designation "redhead." "It's not red, it's orange," he would say. He knew he was a Gingy. I loved our bedtime ritual, milky, 3 books, and then I sang in my softest voice, *Our Song* by Elton John. I had dreamed for many years and told myself that if I was ever so lucky to be a mom, I would sing this song to my child every night, the last words that they will hear from me before they go to sleep.

He chose what he loved with as fierce a will as he had chosen his own birth date. Animals and trains. He was transfixed by the television series Planet Earth. Each week, we'd watch herds of elephants storming the African Plains, sea life teeming below the surface, flocks of birds converging and dispersing. We took nature treks around our neighborhood, with me or Andre pulling Alec in the red Radio Flyer wagon. We'd spot geckos, jackrabbits, hawks, road runners. Anything that moved in the desert caught his eye and captured his imagination. One morning we awoke to a family of javelinas in our driveway, and Alec was in hog heaven. Porky, Mr. Chubs, Bacon Bits... he named them all.

Andre took Alec fishing, embracing that generations old ritual of father-son time all the more because Andre's own father left him as a child. When they couldn't get out to the lake, we made a regular pilgrimage to the Bass Pro Shop—seventeen thousand square feet of outdoor adventure indoors. Andre would boost Alec on his knee so our son could watch the catfish, bass and bluegills circle in the giant freshwater aquarium. Alec loved the 1:30 trout feeding, tossing handfuls of fish food into the manmade stream and watching the trout zoom toward the food—something that somehow, he, a small boy, had set in motion. He'd cast his eye

up through the vast space, taking in and identifying the life-size animals (and animal heads) on display.

As many a great explorer before him, Alec was also fascinated by trains. His passion started with Thomas the Tank Engine and extended to our local train park, McCormick-Stillman. No matter how many times before we had ridden the train around the park, he would still bounce with excitement each time he heard "All Aboard" and the telltale clanging that meant we were off. He loved the model train bunkhouse, with the complex dimensionality of the real world, loops and layers of trains snaking over tracks, across bridges, through tunnels, into stations. Past houses and saloons and shops. Past trees and barns and farms. Carrying coal, carrying passengers through factory towns, oil towns, ranch towns. Alec had befriended many of the volunteers who built these worlds, and they would wave us into a secret entrance to get a close-up viewing.

On the home front, he loved all things Thomas (and Percy, Edward and James). Every birthday, every Chanukah, every special occasion, he added to his train collection. He wore his orange Thomas shirt as many days in a row as I would let him, and he wore those green Thomas pajamas until they were rags. And two sizes too small. He staged an Alec-scale protest when I tried to retire them. In a panic because I couldn't find another pair, I sent an emergency APB email to family and friends to see if anyone could locate more—and allow us all to finally get some sleep at night.

I love being a mom, everything about it, the masterpieces of art that made it to the refrigerator door, the tantrums because he wants to stay at the park longer, the snuggles while we are reading a book, diapers and potty training, I wouldn't trade it for the world. I love being Alec's mom.

In his Thomas the Tank Engine t-shirt, nineteen-month-old Alec was reciting for the record the identifying characteristics of the trains he held in each hand. "Thomas is blue," he said, holding up his left hand. "Percy is green."

He took a few steps across the grass and laid both trains before the headstone. "For them to play with," he said.

I had explained that we were going to a special place to see the memory of our two little girls who came before him but were no longer here and loved us very much. "This is where the babies who are in Heaven go to sleep?" Alec said. "Well, sort of, Mumsie, this is a place where we can visit them". Given how much they loved us, Alec offered his most prized possessions.

This family gathering at the cemetery had been a long time coming. Finally, five years after we left the hospital with a receipt for a burial plot rather than with two babies, I was able to make good on my promise to the twins who were never born. Finally, with Alec fully here, alive and well, I was able to visit their graves and thank them for first making me a mother.

That day came back to me—and the months before it, when Andre and I were, for a brief time, parents of twin girls. The pregnancy that had felt so right, so easy, so natural, that I began to flout long-held Jewish customs ingrained in me by my mother and grandmother. By superstition, Jews avoid attention to the unborn lest they draw the "evil eye." In other words, don't count your chickens before they're hatched. Don't, for instance, pass whole afternoons in Baby's-R-Us buying cribs and a rocker. Don't trade in the sedan for an SUV. Don't list favorite "A" names and "J" names before those chickens are hatched.

Andre had been right there with me, carrying as much of the pregnancy as a father could. It seems like yesterday when he would spread stretch-mark cream on my stomach and whisper to the bump, "You girls behave in there. I'll take care of your mama out here." He spoke a little about his father, who'd left him and his mother when he was a baby. He would never do that, he said, relishing the chance to break the cycle, to raise his kids with the love and reliability that his father never stuck around to show him. I remember when the beginning of the end came on that sunny, pregnant afternoon in a long line of them. The sudden drop. Six months after I lost the girls, they went on to—I believe—save my life from Hodgkin's lymphoma.

"Thank you," I whispered to the girls now. "For saving my life." I looked at the bright blue and green smiling trains standing incongruously in front of the headstone. "And for this." I knelt behind Alec and put my arms around him, his spun-copper hair looking impossibly rare and valuable in the sun. Alec turned around and gently grabbed my face, "Mom, sing the babies our song, that's the song that you sing when your babies are going to sleep". It was as if God himself was speaking through Alec. I have my girls, I have my boy, my health, a family. I was blind, but now I see. I get it, now I really get it.

Thank you. I can't believe that made it.

FOR RICHER OR POORER

*Forgiveness simply means loving yourself and others
enough to pursue healing instead of punishment.*

- Barbara Ann Kipfer

WEEKENDS WERE FILLED with trips to the train park, DQ Blizzards, swimming lessons and endless construction of Thomas the Train tracks across the house. We were having the time of our lives, life was perfect, until the brick wall. While Alec was happy and healthy, my six-year marriage was not. I knew Andre had alcoholism in his family. And I knew, truth be told, that he was drinking too much. I am a licensed social worker, and am board certified in addictions, but I also know human nature: the closer we stand to someone, the more difficult it is to see them clearly.

He was functioning fine—no missed work, no slurred words or bursts of anger, was it all me? Am I just too sensitive or prudish? He would grow mellow in the evening, not absent, just subdued. But the quantity he consumed was unmistakable and concerning. Two martinis every night, three on weekends. Massive ones. One night when we found ourselves having the same regurgitated conversation around his drinking, I measured out the shots with water in front of him and made my point even more forcefully than I'd intended: each drink held eight ounces of gin. Times two drinks, or three. Times seven days a week. He agreed. He justified. Or apologized. In the end, it always was the same, he pointed out that he was functioning just fine so it didn't matter. And he continued to drink.

Still, I was not prepared for the admission I got one morning after I had returned from a conference in Boston. "Wow, someone must have really not been paying attention or driving way too fast", I said as Andre and I pulled into the back gate of our housing development. Silence. I ran inside to greet my beautiful orange haired boy when Andre sat down in Alec's room and began to cry. We were together in Alec's room as our son busied himself with the new toy car I had brought him from my trip. Andre was rocking back and forth nervously in the rocking chair. "I did something bad, really bad", Andre said. I couldn't imagine what it was, as Alec was right in front of me, healthy, happy, safe. "I got drunk while you were away." He blinked tears. "I crashed the car into the brick wall." My eye went right to Alec, who was clearly unhurt as he blithely rolled his new toy around the room. A part of me breathed a sigh of relief. I had known that Andre's drinking had increased, but he always rebuffed my awareness, "I only drink 2 martinis". What he failed to recognize is that the glasses held 8 shots of alcohol. It's over, the gig is up, he has an alcohol problem and it no longer was the dynamic of my perception vs his, the DUI spoke for itself. I put my arms around him and told him that we can get help, being a board-certified addiction counselor, this was my bailiwick. "Um, there was someone else in the car," Andre said. Another woman. A prostitute. He may have called her an escort, but I didn't need a translation.

My initial, visceral response was "get out of the house". How could he do this to our family? He had left Alec essentially alone in the house (our live-in nanny was in her room, but she was off duty after 7 p.m.). What had he risked? What had he exposed us to? I never wanted to see him again. In my suspended state of disbelief, I was suddenly overcome by a wave of relief. I am done. No more arguing over drinking, no more watching the glass, calibrating the bottle. It was as if the crash had gone right through our marriage, and I was on the other side. Alone and apart.

"It was only once," he pleaded. "We didn't even do anything. We never even made it back to the house."

Never made it back to the house—where our son was sleeping—because he was drunk and crashed the car. That was supposed to make it better? As I would come to learn, he was giving me two sides of himself at once. Often one was hidden, though its shadow could be felt, like the dark side of the moon. I told the nanny, in tears, that Andre had done something horrible and that she is in charge of Alec, I will be back. I don't even remember the drive to William and Ronnie's house They knew already, Andre had called them the day it happened and confessed. So here I was, at a crossroads: stay with an alcoholic who brings home prostitutes or leave. I asked Andre to leave, I could do this, we can sell the house, share custody and he can live the life he wants. He left for about 5 days, until one day he showed up at dinnertime. "What are you doing here?", I asked. "I'm not leaving, if you don't want to be with me, then you get out". His unbelievable arrogance repulses me to this day. I loved him and I hated him. I had friends who were advising me to leave. I had family—notably, my parents, who loved Andre like a son, reminding me that alcoholism is a biological and psychological illness—advising me to stay if Andre was willing to get help. Something they said as they talked to us on a visit three weeks later resonated deeply: "You don't get to choose how your partner makes mistakes." They had been married for almost fifty years, so they had some standing here.

I was not going to leave Alec with him, no way, not with an active alcoholic, not with hookers, not a chance. If I had to suck it up and stay with him in the house in order to have some semblance of knowledge and control over my son's welfare and home, I will. So that is what I did. It is almost impossible not to cloud this juncture with the terrible clarity of hindsight. But at the time, we were indeed partners. We had our ups and downs, but we were family, Andre and I. He had made a giant mistake. Maybe even an unforgivable one. He knew it, and I knew it. But having recently undergone a year of difficult but ultimately successful treatment for cancer, I knew a thing or two about fighting malignancy. After having suffered through miscarriage, infertility and, even with surrogacy, a dangerously premature birth, I also knew a thing or two about second chances. So, we did all we could to get our marriage back.

We went to couples counseling for eighteen months, and Andre talked a good game. He thanked God for intervening, crashing the current dangerous course he was on so he could get on a better track. I listened, I hoped, I believed. We fought so hard to get this family off the ground that I was determined to keep it together, ragged as it was right now. Initially, there was a considerable part of me that did not want to get back together, but we just needed to learn how to be civil to each other. I also wanted to know what happened, what was the matter with him and what was his intentions in treating his alcoholism. Week in, week out, we sat on Dr. Mayer's couch. Part of me wanted to leave this relationship, but I realized that just because this happened, did not make the part of me that loved being a family go away. So, I hung in there. I chose to champion him. I didn't get to choose if he was an alcoholic but it was my choice if I wanted to be with someone who was in recovery, helping himself, getting better.

Around Thanksgiving, we had to meet with Andre's attorney, one of many lovely consequences of the DUI. When we were called into the attorney's office, Andre and I got up, but he quickly turned and asked me to stay in the waiting room. Why? What the hell is this? Why would I be sequestered from a part of this meeting? I thought he told me everything, wasn't that the premise of our counseling? No secrets? He reappeared about 5 minutes later to retrieve me. I sat through that meeting as if I was hollowed. "Do you want to tell me what that was about?". Here it goes, another confession : " I have been driving around on a suspended license". "I'm sorry, what? Since when? Don't you know that you could be jailed for that? Or lose your license indefinitely and cost our family a lot more money that we don't have? What would happen to Alec if he had to be taken by the police because you were arrested?". I had had it. I am so tired of his contemptuous attitude towards the law and our safety, for honesty. I want a divorce. I'm out of here. Here we go again. "Give me another chance". I was so angry that we had deposited so much love, dreams, future plans, goals into our emotional bank account, because now it is so hard to pull out. F**k it, I have to stay. This is the only way that I can protect my son, my beautiful Alec. I would rather take a chance with future lies than to risk not knowing what is going on or who is caring for him. I was willing to make that sacrifice. We would sell our house, sell the cars, let go of the nanny, do what we have to do. If I was to stay, I would make the best of it. I can't control if Andre lied or told the truth, that could happen in a marriage or divorce. For richer or poorer, I was in.

With a DUI conviction, Andre had his driver's license suspended, so we made some changes. We sold our dream house in the mountains and moved closer to town and Alec's school. Andre rode our son to school on his bicycle. Unable to continue as a real estate agent without a car, Andre began stock-trading from home. I worked harder. We had a little savings and a 401K. He stayed sober. We had our health. We had our son. And that was enough.

"I told you, I'm only going to do this once, I will never get a divorce", Andre said. Those words resonate in my head. At the time when he said them, I interpreted them as a symbol of the depth of his commitment, divorce was not an alternative no matter what. Now I see that there was a different meaning, I had lacked the receptor to decode his cryptic belief, until death do we part. He wasn't going to permit a divorce and would punish me if I ever wanted to. There it is, that is the crux of killing the boys. How could I have ever decoded that?

MIRACLE BOY

*The secret to happiness is that it is always a
choice and depends on ourselves.*

- Aristotle

THIS FEELING WAS hauntingly familiar: run down, dizzy, nauseous. Please, I prayed, don't let it be cancer again. I have my Alec. I cannot leave him. With familiar dread, I headed back to the doctor.

Life on life's terms, I tried to remind myself as I had so many times before. Whatever the diagnosis was, we would get through it. It seemed like forever until the doctor came into my exam room. Deep breath, whatever he has to tell me, I can do this. The future is none of my business, uncontrollable, the only thing that I can control is what I decide to do about it, whatever *it* is. Here it comes.

"You're pregnant," the doctor said.

"What? Me?", I thought to myself, "you must have the wrong dipstick because that is impossible. I have only one fallopian tube, a weak cervix and an immune system sure to sink a pregnancy".

"Are you sure?", I responded. "How could this have happened? I mean, I know how it happened but how did it happen?".

I guess the doctors sometimes don't know everything and certainly the body is unpredictable.

With great caution, we took home our news. I must have stared at the ultrasound picture a hundred times that night. Pregnant. Well I guess something was growing inside of me, I just didn't think it would be a baby. I was waiting for it though, the blood in the toilet, the loss. I am not a nay-sayer but when the earth has opened up in front of you twice, it becomes a question of when, not if.

Well versed in the caprices of pregnancy, we told no one, not even Alec. So, I don't know how to explain how my almost-four-year-old came to put his hand on my not-yet-showing belly, eleven weeks into pregnancy, and said, "Mommy, my baby's in here." Andre and I just looked at each other, mystified. The only way I can explain this is by looking back, knowing what I know now: they are spirits joined together for eternity, before and after this life.

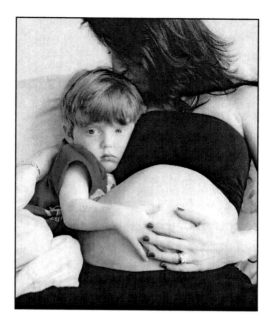

This pregnancy was so different from the last one. I was no longer buoyant and effusive about my cravings, my growing belly, my love of "A" names, my vision for the future nursery. I focused instead on the visceral and intimate details of my body, attending constantly to how often and in which direction the baby moved, any internal shifting, the tiniest spot of blood. I was under close watch of my perinatologist,

Dr. Perlow, what a gentle man. At our first meeting, he mapped it out for us, one week at a time. He put me on progesterone in addition to the standard prenatal vitamins, securing all of our bases. At fifteen weeks, I had a cerclage, in layman's terms, the doctor "sewed him in," stitching the cervix so the baby would stay put. My twins may have been too much for my uterus, but nothing would escape me again. Not on my watch. The high light of my day was when I got to check off another day that I got to be pregnant on the calendar, marked by the weeks/days, just like the board at the hospital where I delivered the girls, 11:4, 11:5, 11:6, 12:1. 14 weeks, I am safe. Right?

My mother came to help out so I could stay off my feet. I spoke to my dad every day—as a supportive father but also as a longtime OB/GYN who asked for and evaluated the daily nuances of pregnancy, adding greatly to my peace of mind. I loved lying in bed, spending my days when I wasn't working, holding my growing belly, talking to Asher and dreaming of his arrival. I relished every moment, knowing that I was given another miracle baby. With Alec, Andre took the lead so I could rest. He eagerly awaited his second son and carried an ultrasound picture of the growing baby in his wallet. Another boy to take to the train park and the Bass Pro Shop. Another future builder of railroad tracks, hider-and-seeker, fisherman, catcher and thrower of balls.

Unlike Alec, who couldn't wait to come into the world and did so at thirty-three weeks, Asher Samuel was content to stay. Dr. Perlow's plan was to cut the cerclage at 37 weeks, he was measuring at 8 1/2 pounds and would be mature enough to sustain on his own, no NIC-U, no preemie clothes. Well that didn't go as planned, not in the way that we are familiar with. Asher had other ideas, he wanted to stay with me. And stay he did until the doctors forced him out at thirty-eight weeks and almost ten pounds to ensure his safe delivery. I tried so hard to get that big baby out but just couldn't. The attending obstetrician looked at my father (yes, he was in the delivery room), with respect for a wise man, "Dr. Zellner?". My Dad said, "3 more chances". Three pushes later, no chance. It all happened so quickly, I was wheeled into the OR and 5 minutes later, Andre was handing me our miracle. "Look Laur, it's Ashie" he said beaming. My mother swears he finally came out because he heard the word "lunch." Then there was Alec. His first words when he saw Ashie had a resounding "told you so" tone. "See Mom, I told you my baby was in there. I'll never leave my baby". I didn't quite know what he meant, but I would soon find out.

It was all worth it, the chemotherapy, the bone pain, the hair loss, the blood transfusions, the decision to stay. There is no clinical or empirically based explanation to explain nor understand how this came to be, I just like to believe that the spirits of my girls were and are the souls of Alec and Asher. They always knew of their return to me, it just wouldn't be then, in those bodies. I was not privy to this celestial plan, so masterly orchestrated, but now I see it clearly. I guess it's true what they say...Man plans, God laughs.

Two beautiful children, miracle boys.

Now I see it, the Color Pink is the Color Blue.

THE BIG, BAD WOLF

*Our true enemies are the mental poisons of ignorance,
hatred, desire, jealousy and pride. They are the only
things capable of destroying our happiness.*

- Barbara Ann Kipfer

LIFE FOR OUR FAMILY was finally a joyous one, at least I thought
so for me and my boys. I had returned to the hospital, case
managing the cardiac unit and the ICU and Alec was having a
blast introducing his new baby brother to all of his teachers and
friends at their preschool. For once in a long time, I felt like the
storm had passed and we were on stable ground. Andre had been
continuing his real estate sales and began dabbling in day trading and seemed to find genuine happiness, without alcohol. He
seemed to resemble the man that I fell in love with. At least I
thought he was.

Rome began to crumble when we decided to apply for a home
mortgage loan, remodification, interest rates were at an all-time
low and we were one of the many that felt the crash of the Phoenix housing bubble. I remember so clearly, calling Andre into the
office in an alarming fashion as I pulled up our 401K account in
preparing our loan package.

"Andre, there's something really off with this account, we need to call the bank right away, all of our money is missing., it says we only have $2766.04?".

He knew right then and there that I had stumbled upon something, a bone that he had buried in the hope that it would never surface. I have seen that look before.

"Andre, what the f**k is going on?".

" I made a mistake. I was day trading and I entered into this reverse trade and it was called and I...".

"What are you saying? You gambled away our entire savings on a trade? Are you ,insane, there was $180,000 in that account!? What are you saying, all of our money is gone?"

Red, that is all I saw. I can't take it, if it's not one thing, it's another. Lying. Escort. Alcoholism. Now Gambling our savings? Alec's college fund? I can't do this anymore. No more. How many more times can I look past this destructive behavior and continue to be a party to it? It is now destroying me, my future, the future of the children. It was clear that this man had a deep psychological deficit, a fissure in his personality that was incongruent with the goals that I had for myself and my future, for who I wanted as a partner. He didn't need to promise, plead or correct anything anymore. This was between Andre and himself, I no longer had anything to fight for. I was clear that we would be able to live apart, I was no longer willing to have my house blown away time after time like the three little pigs. We would both be able to love these boys and co-parent these boys, but being partners was no longer. Silence. There was a lot of silence. I needed to be quiet so that I could get clarity of what this division and separation was going to look like.

Weeks went by, laden with Andre's pleas and plans to get back the money, but it was too late. You can't un-ring a bell. Period. I spent the next two months picking up extra shifts at the hospital and picked up a part-time on call position for a crisis line, anything that I could do to squirrel away nuts for the cold winter to come. He begged me to go back to Dr. Mayer with him so we can *work it out*. Work it out? How? What could there possibly be to work out? That's like trying to rebuild the World Trade Center after it fell. I didn't know what I wanted to do but I knew what I didn't want and that was more of this.

I don't know what possessed me to ask him that night after we put the boys to sleep but it just came out, a statement rather than a question that I had broached many times in Dr. Mayer's office over our numerous counseling sessions. I was not expecting what came next.

"I know it was not the first escort that you had been with, I know that there were more".

"You're right." he said quietly as if he were at confession.

"What?", I thought to myself. "He wasn't supposed to say that?". I got up in disbelief and went to sleep in Alec's room. As I laid there stroking those beautiful orange stands of hair, theories of why he had decided to tell me flooded my brain. Why now? He could have continued to lie and I probably would have never known. Maybe he was engaging in prostitutes again and it was just a matter of time before I found out. Or maybe he decided to make a pact with himself and live an honest life? No, I got it, maybe he knew that I was done, that the financial ruin was the final straw that broke the back of this relationship. He had nothing to lose by coming clean. Maybe he was being blackmailed, maybe all of the money that he "said" he lost went to pay off the whores who are threatening to blow the whistle on him? I reflected on the past 18 months, week after week on the couch in Dr. Mayer's office discussing trust and transparency and all along, he still wasn't willing to come clean. I feel like such a fool. I guess he is a person who is unwilling, unable or incapable of taking personal responsibility, there isn't any psychological mystery, this is what it boils down to.

The next morning was different, any thread that tied me to this man anymore was severed and it was palatable.

"Twenty-seven", he said as I poured myself a cup of coffee.

"Twenty-seven what?", I asked.

"Escorts. That's how many I was with".

I put my coffee down, it was as if the world stopped turning and spun off its axis. I couldn't say anything. My brain is not processing this information. Thoughts are exploding; why would you need to go to prostitutes? What diseases are you carrying? What could you have possibly passed on to me? When did you find the time to do it? Where? In my bed? In my home? And why are you tracking the number? What is that about? Who was watching the boys when you were doing this? Is this where our savings went to? My brain is swirling, I have to go. I have to get out of here. I have to go to work. I went upstairs and kissed my sleeping boys with tears in my eyes. OK Laurie, suck it up, we have to go downstairs, put on a straight face and get your game face on for work. No drama, there will be time later, right now we need to just do what is in front of us and that's to get out of the house so you can clear your mind and drive to work.

Andre was still standing in the kitchen at the same place when he dropped the bomb on me.

"I will pick the boys up today, we can discuss this later", I said as I left.

That day was a haze for me, it is kind of like when you are day dreaming and kind of drift off, except I am not dreaming, it is a nightmare. I have so many decisions to make. I lasted as long as I could in this relationship. It's over. My partner Tricia was amazing, I was useless at the hospital and she directed me to take care of business. I needed to plan my next move. An apartment. A bank account. An exit.

The next weeks were filled with him pleading for me to forgive him, he swore that this was in the past and that "he has been *good* for 2 years". He tried over countless discussions, over and over, about his twenty-seven prostitutes and that he was "really coming clean now", no more secrets. He cried that he was an alcoholic and sex addict and that I should understand, given my training in addictions. As for me, I didn't care. I understood addictions, but he was not my patient and I choose not to live with active addiction. I don't want it. I was resigned, my questions were pointed and strategic, I wanted to know exactly how far his deviant behavior extended. It was as if I was collecting this information to ensure that all bridges were blown up, there was no re- entering this relationship, under no circumstance.

It turned out that Andre would hire these women and meet them at an apartment complex in North Scottsdale. Apparently, there is a network where prostitutes rent 2-or 3- bedroom apartments and reserve the bedrooms for their appointments, sort of like a shared office space. He would have these rendezvous when I was at work and after he dropped the children off at school, he would have sex with them when he was sitting open houses and also tell listing agents that he had potential clients that he wanted to show property to. His behavior was stripped of any ethic or semblance of propriety. He didn't care about me, the boys, his license, the other people's homes, the law, our future. He was careless, and I mean care-less. Without a care for anyone or anything.

It is not my most "Buddhist" moment, but I have something to say to this person, this person who once looks like the man that I married, but at the same time, is a complete foreigner to me. I lit into him…

"There is plenty of therapy that I could go through to resolve my anger, disappointment and disgust with you, but the one aspect that I cannot forgive you for is this…You took my health into your own hands. I fought my ass off to not die from cancer, and you have some nerve carelessly exposing my health to a hooker who God knows what biology she has swirling around inside her? And then you bring that home to me?! You like getting f**ked? Well it is not me that did this to you, you f**ked yourself". So, give me some time and space to figure out this f*ing mess that you dropped in my lap, just leave me to my thoughts and give me space to digest this.

But he couldn't do that, the anticipation of what I was thinking or what I was going to do was increasing his desperation and his suspicions.

One day, shortly after our confrontation, I received a text from AT &T while at work, notifying me that my cell number had been added to the "family plan location services app". My disposition of feeling baffled and concerned quickly shifted to suspicion.

"Do you know what this app notice is?", I asked Andre when I got home.

"No, what is it?".

"Huh, OK, well I don't know what it is either. I'm going to call AT&T to make sure no one has tapped into our account or that we are not being charged for a service that we didn't sign up for".

"Wait, I know what it is", he said. "I did it. I put a location tracking program on your phone so I can see where you are".

"You what? You are tracking *me*, like I am some animal on a safari?"

*He has some nerve, tracking me, as if I was the one who had breached the trust in our relationship? I wasn't the one who f*cked 27 hookers", I thought to myself. "Un-f*cking believable!".*

I had had it. I am done, there is no more time to ponder the possibility of living in the same house until we sell it and then separate, I need to move away and quickly. I proceeded with my exit strategy but with that, came increasing anger and desperation from Andre. He knew that I was slipping away from his persuasive grip and there wasn't anything to do to stop me. I no longer wanted to understand what he wanted me to understand, I was clear on what is, and what is, is a man who wants to live his life contrary to mine. I needed to set up my next lily pad but needed some time. After I put the boys down to sleep, I would quietly announce that I was going to clear my head. I spent countless hours driving around or walking around the block, thinking about the past, the future and what is best for us. I wanted to find a place that felt like home, a place where the boys could play outdoors to run and play and not be cooped up, I wanted to be able to have room to spread out our train tracks and construct our imaginary racetracks, I wanted the least amount of disruption as possible.

I remember that exact moment when I knew that time was up, when the alarm went off. I needed to leave and leave quickly; the decision had been made for me. Andre and I put the boys down to sleep, separately of course. I came downstairs and was in the office, working on some charts, he was in and out, pleading for me to talk to him and asking me to stay. This was unproductive and seemingly escalating, I couldn't concentrate and reached my capacity of interruptions and badgering. I said good night and headed up to Alec's room, I was sleeping in his room for obvious reasons, unbeknownst to him.

"You know what, why don't you just leave now, just get out", Andre said as I walked up the stairs.

"Andre, let's just go to sleep".

"No, you have a choice, you can get out now or I'll call the cops and they will remove you".

I couldn't believe that this was happening, all of the sudden, my husband, my friend, was this indistinguishable aggressor. I continued to go to Alec's room where I quietly called my neighbor Wendi from Alec's closet, she lived adjacent from us and I knew that she would be able to see if he followed through on his threat.

"Don't worry honey, he's just bullying you, he's not going to call the cops and drag you out of your house with your kids sleeping at 11:00 p.m. Wait, oh shit, there are lights in front of your house, son of a bitch, he did it, he called the cops on you", she said.

I have never had a confrontation with the police in my life, God, I am petrified. I stood very still on Alec's bed in my pajamas, "please don't come up here, please don't take me away". And amongst all of this, laid my beautiful gingy boy, dreaming away while, in the meantime, I just entered a nightmare. There was a knock on the bedroom door. I opened it.

"Mrs. Leteve? Good evening, I'm officer Talbot. What seems to be going on here tonight?".

I told him what was going on and what had transpired over the past 3 weeks, the short version.

"Well if he doesn't want to be around you, then he can leave".

I sighed. I'm not going to be kicked out. I don't have to leave my kids. But what would happen once the police leave? If he could do this, what else would he try to do? Maybe he will throw my stuff out on the front lawn, maybe he will take out all of the money in our checking accounts or block the credit cards? Thank God he is not a violent person, at least I don't have to deal with that. But calling the cops? It was obvious that he was going to try to use the law to get back at me, for what crime I committed, who knows? I locked both doors to Alec's room and stacked up blocks in front of the door, so if he tried to enter in the middle of the night, the noise would signal me, my mock intruder alarm. I am so thankful that Alec is a heavy sleeper, but it's clear, we can't stay here, I need to set up our next lily pad and quick.

He confirmed it, he wasn't going to play nice.

THE COTTAGE AND THE EGG COLLECTION

Wealth is the number of things one can do without.

- Anonymous

THIS DAY IS A BLUR to me, it's surreal. Moving Day. After the police fiasco, we both knew that separation would be the necessary next step. I would have asked him to leave the house, but of course, I already knew what his disposition would be, one of two options: angry and hostile or teary and begging. When I announced that I was moving out, it was forced off of my tongue, not because I wanted to stay but because I was afraid of the verbal backlash that I thought was waiting for me on the other side of the conversation. To my surprise, he was quiet. We agreed upon the day and conditions, I was only going to take my clothes, toiletries, half of the boys' clothes and toys, the portable crib for Ashie and a few pictures. It's amazing, after all of the time and attention one puts into growing and nurturing a relationship, which really is a living, breathing organism created by two people, the dissolution is reduced down to three things: possessions, money and children. That's it, regardless of race, socio-economics, how long the marriage lasted or how many kids. All of the sudden, things, friends, parenting time is dived up like pie at Thanksgiving. It was not an easy decision, but a clear one. I remember listening to a YouTube video on the Dalai Lama talking about divorce, I will never forget his response to a very young girl who talked about just this type of situation, she and her young husband had just stopped growing, she wanted to know what to do. The Dalai Lama said matter of factly – "well, divorce of course, why would you stay?" Stunned silence inside of me. Has He gone mad? Then it sunk in, of course, it was obvious. I had stopped growing. He had stopped growing. I could not grow in this ecosystem. It also made clear that when someone is in a relationship with chemicals, there is an inability to grow. There wasn't any other option for me.

On the day of the move, Andre in his fashion, decided to change the locks to the house. Lovely, I was locked out of my own house. If I needed any further confirmation whether I was making the right decision for myself, I needed nothing further. I am so glad that William and Ronnie were there to help me move, it was a very strange dynamic that seemed to fall quickly over us. It was as if we were actors in a horror movie, scampering and scurrying around the house to quickly gather our handful of possessions before the villain arrived home. Three cars filled up to the top, we had done it. I was officially out; the rest of the possessions could be determined in our decree. These remaining objects really were of secondary concern, I could take them or leave them, they were just objects that hold memories, stories of our stories. I have never really been attached to objects, especially since the cancer. Objects are just that, objects. I never once said throughout my entire bout with cancer, that I wish I had more things, more trinkets, a bigger house or more furniture. What came into clarity was the importance of two things, time and people. And all I ever wanted was more time with the people who I love. So, take the stuff, the couches, the art, it is all replaceable, it's the boys and my health that matters and I have both.

My friend Christopher, I call him Sweet Christopher, found us a two-bedroom patio home for rent, it was furnished, affordable, near the hospital and most importantly, it was peaceful. I didn't have to worry about what I was coming home to, be it a man desperately following me around the house asking for forgiveness, threats or another confession.

Alec loved our new space, Ashie was of course clueless at 9 months old, but Alec owned it. He immediately began setting up his tracks and helped me set up his room. I had something new to bring to this nest, eggs. Alec had become fascinated with dinosaurs, turtles, all living things, how things evolved and came into being. When I brought Alec into his new room, his eyes lit up. I had dedicated an entire shelf to eggs, Ostrich eggs, alligator eggs, duck eggs, peahens and the like. I even had a nurse who owned a farm give me an Emu egg (these are a teal color). Alec threw his arms around me and gave me a big hug, " These are awesome Mom!".

He glanced over his shoulder at me as he admired these magical shells.

"Mom, do you remember what Mr. and Mrs. Bird said in our book, *The Best Nest?* Well I think this is the best nest". I smiled with pride. *This is home, this feeling is what home is,* I thought as I put his new Lightning McQueen bed spread on his bed.

"But why did we need another house?", he asked.

God, why does he have to be so wise? I thought to myself as I kneeled down.

"I have to be close to the hospital right now, Mumsie (that's a nickname for Alec), Daddy is going to be at the other house until we sort some things out. But I need for you to remember 3 things, OK?: 1) your job is to have fun, no matter what you are doing, 2) be kind and 3) learn, about everything and anything that you want, that's it baby. Can you do that?". I said.

"Sure Mom, that's easy".

I was so afraid of how and what to share with Alec about this new home, the shuffling back and forth, the new routines... that's the best that I came up with. I don't think that there is any amount of preparation that one can have to recite to their kids the information bomb of a divorce.

It was all worth it. I loved our new nest, I made sure that some of our favorite things didn't get left at the other house, such as having dance parties (just the 3 of us turning on the music and dancing like fools in our living room, showing off impromptu made up moves, mine of course had to include holding Ashie), pillow fights, track building, walking to get ice cream and hunting for geckos, and feeding the ducks at the near-by lake. We were going to be just fine, I am sure that the initial separation of any marriage is hard, but things will settle down: so I thought.

I returned home one Sunday night from dinner with the boys to find a person standing at my garage door.

"Can I help you?", I asked as I pulled up.

"Are you Laurie Leteve?", they asked.

I acknowledged and quickly put two and two together that they were a process server, but not for the divorce papers. I opened up the envelope to find that Andre had petitioned the Court to gain emergency physical custody of the children. He was trying to take the boys away from me. I read further, his reasoning is that he believes that I am going to take the boys back to Florida to live. Kidnapping? Is he crazy? Where is he coming up with this stuff? I read further to see when the hearing is. Tomorrow? The court day was tomorrow? I rushed into the house and feverishly called my attorney Mr. Jensen. Pick up, pick up, please, pick up.

"Hello?", he answered. *Thank God.* I haven't felt this much panic since the day when I got the call from Traci that Alec was on his way. I had my boys and now they were going to be taken from me? I mean it's one thing that my girls were taken from me by God, by nature, but by a person? "He has no case Laurie, he can say whatever he wants, it is ridiculous and unfounded. Fax me the paperwork and I'll see you in the morning". That night I tried so hard to be present, but my mind took me into court, stories swirling in my head. Will I lose my kids tomorrow? Will the Judge believe his preposterous theory? How the hell could he accuse me of wanting to leave the state? I have lived here for 25 years, I have my license here, my friends, my practice? Wait. I know where he got this from. He is pissed because he is not going on the family cruise. He was disinvited after the police stunt. Of course, he is skewing my upcoming Miami trip with the entire family to celebrate Aunt Linda and Uncle Joel's fortieth wedding anniversary, to seem as if I am leaving the State never to return. What an asshole, he was the one who decided to call the cops on me and kick me out of my own house. When I told him that it was best to not come on the cruise, he sought revenge. He reminds me so much of this girl that I used to go to high school with. She was not a kind person, I had no idea what her beef was with me and why she did not like me, but she would relentlessly gossip about me. I get that sometimes people just don't like people, but this world is big enough for all of us. Why do others feel the need to intentionally hurt others just because they don't like them? I never understood this concept, I still don't. OK, come here Laurie, to this moment. You have your two beautiful boys in front of you right now, come here, with them. Fear was in my every cell. I guess tomorrow will be born in its own time.

Tomorrow we will see…

I brought the boys to school the next morning, holding back tears as I gave them hugs and kisses, not knowing if I would be allowed to pick them up after school. When I would see them again? I never wish this feeling upon any parent, that feeling of separation from their kids, of your fate being determined by another. Please let the Judge see the truth of what is.

Court was interesting, it is so surreal to see the person that you loved in the opposing table, no eye contact, now he is a Plaintiff and I, a Respondent. Mr. Jensen was stellar, he was an older gentleman, about 70 years old, he reminded me of a sweet grandfather, but if you pissed him off, he would nail your ass to the wall. Andre decided to represent himself. What is that old adage, "He who represents himself has a fool for a client?". That's what I think, but knowing Andre and his seemingly new arrogance, he thought by reading about divorce courts on the internet, that he could litigate his own case. The judge read the motion for emergency custody and heard evidence very quickly from Mr. Jensen, the contrary. Dismissed. As we were walking out of the courtroom, Mr. Jensen let Andre know that he may want to reconsider formal legal representation, that the goal is to keep this as amicable as possible.

"Whatever Grandpa, you just worry about yourself. I know what I am doing.", remarked Andre.

"Well, if that is the direction you want to go, then rest assured that your drinking, the 27 hookers and your gambling will be fair game", Jensen said.

Oh God, I just wanted to run away, I didn't want a fight, I just don't want to be married to him anymore. He is the one who has trespassed all over this relationship and now that I want to move away, he is angry and playing the victim? Unbelievable. Well, I guess someone has to get an ugly divorce, we got it. Jensen will be worth every penny that I give him, as long as I have my boys...

THE VIRGIN MARY

*I do not believe in a fate that falls on men how-
ever they act; but I do believe in a fate that falls
on them unless they act.*

- Buddha

AUGUST 2009

It was a typical day on the cardiac care floor and I was busy buzzing around our triangle shaped unit, when I noticed a man come onto the unit. Now being a case manager, we are always strategically aware of who enters our units, if it's a physician, we want to review clinical status, if it's a family member, we want to discuss discharge planning, and if it's a stranger, well, we are aware of who is visiting our patients. Either way you slice it, we know what's up. I didn't recognize him, but I must admit, did take notice that he was very handsome. I finished entering my note and proceeded to the nurses' station to conduct clinical rounds with my favorite nurse,

Yelena, I call her "Mother Russia" of our floor because of her experience and thick, accent.

"OK, ah Laurie, he a needs a case management" Yelena said in her thick accent as she pointed in the direction of the handsome, gentleman who I noted entering the unit before. I walked up to him.

"Do you need case management?

"Um yes".

"OK, what do you need?".

"Well, tell me about what case management is, maybe I will need it?".

Yelena quickly jumped in, as if all of the sudden, my yenta fairy godmother descended.

"Laurie, this is Dr. Morales, Dr. Morales, this is Laurie". "Nice to meet you Dr. Morales, I haven't seen you here before, are you new?"

"No, I mostly practice at Mayo Hospital or at the Osborn campus. I never come to this campus, but I guess it was my luck".

"Are you a cardiologist?"

"Nephrology". Kidneys.

"Right, so who's beans need your attention?"

"Mr. Gibbs in room 2125".

Oh, I did it. Yelena was pointing to Mr. Gibb's room, not to Dr. McDreamy. Shit. OK, I stepped into that one. Now I know why he was so perplexed when I approached him.

"I apologize, when Yelena pointed in your direction, I assumed that you needed my services. Welcome to the unit, if you need anything, please let me know".

"No, I appreciate your attention. Tell me, what do you do when you are not case managing?"

"It's me and my boys, they are 5 years old and 6 months, you know, trains, bikes, gecko hunting".

"Boys huh, I have two girls, mine are 4 and 2 1/2".

What in the world is going on here, I never, ever have fished from a company peer!? But this guy's is so engaging. I can't do this, it's not right, I am flirting. Is it OK to flirt, after all, I am not yet divorced? Well emotionally, does that count? What's the harm, it's just a benign conversation, it's all just clean fun, then I will assess Mr. Gibbs.

We bantered back and forth, laughing and innocently engaging each other, it's as if the world disappeared around the two of us. Poor Mr. Gibbs, his kidneys would have to wait 5 more minutes.

" Well Laurie Beth, this is really awkward and I have never done this before but would you like to get together some time and talk about life after divorce?".

"That would be nice, thank you".

"Here", he said, as he reached into his pocket and wrote down his cell phone number on the back of his card. "Well Laurie Beth, I hope that you call".

With that, Dr. McDreamy disappeared into Mr. Gibbs's room.

"What?", as I looked at Yelena with a grimace, as if the cat just ate the canary.

Our first date was at this Italian restaurant, nothing fancy, just like Alejandro. Authentic and unassuming. It was a local mom and pop place, where real Italians went to watch soccer while fraternizing with each other at small round tables surrounded by pictures of famous previous visitors and eat amazing food. A place where the phrase, "can I have a side of marinara" is blasphemous. I had him meet me in front of a local grocery store, as I was not ready to have anyone come to my house and certainly not trusting of Andre. I have this lingering suspicion since the cell phone tracking incident, that he would all of the sudden appear to infiltrate any plans that I had.

The conversation was amazing, call it chemistry, pheromones or fate, it was a great evening. I loved learning about him, this man who grew up in Bogota, Colombia at the height of the FARQ and war in his home country, graduating high school at age 15 and then directly to medical school. He had been in the United States to conduct research at Harvard and continued on to practice nephrology at the Cleveland Clinic. He likes to say that he is just a plumber for people. As I said, very humble and unassuming.

New Years Eve, 2009

We talked about our marriages, divorces, kids, life, careers, there was so much that we wanted to learn about each other. Nothing mattered to either of us in that moment, ex-husbands or ex-wives, we both felt as if we were the luckiest people to have found the other. To this day, Alejandro has not been back to the hospital, who knows how this place works, if there was a different detail that would have thrown our trajectory off course, this would not be part of my story. I like to believe that this universe is just so organically synchronized, Alejandro just likes to believe that the Virgin Mary had her fingerprints all over this one. Either way, it felt delicious.

Months went by and Alejandro surprised me with a trip to Hawaii for our fortieth birthdays, we were born 2 days apart, so we have coined October 14th as our birthday. Life was easy, Alec, Ashie and I were settling in to our cabana, as I called our new patio home, work was great and I officially had a boyfriend.

We had the same parenting nights with our children, so every Monday and Tuesdays were off limits, he was with his girls, me with my boys. We had decided after about 4 months to introduce them to each other, the babes were 5yrs,4yrs,3yrs and 6 months, and it was a blast for all. Adele and Alec were the leaders, and Juliet adored lugging around Asher who was about 23 pounds at the time. It was effortless, it didn't matter where we went or what we did, from picnics and art festivals to picking out Halloween pumpkins and impromptu Michael Jackson dance parties.

Our union was not without challenges though, all of the kids were adapting and we were paying attention. One day when we were playing, Adele approached me, Ashie in my one arm and Alec on the side of me. I knew it was just a matter of time.

" You know, you're not my Mom?".

"I know, of course I'm not, you have one, I love that we see things the same. I'm the luckiest girl to be who's Mom?".

"Alec and Ashie", she replied with a smile.

"Right, you see I'm just a person who cares about all of us and wants to have fun with you. Does that sound OK with you?".

Alec chimed in," She's my Mom and Ashie's Mom, we are lucky".

"Yes, (smiling) that sounds good".

"OK, so now that we got that settled, let's go have some fun".

I caught Alejandro looking at me out of the corner of my eye. I turned. "Yes?.", I asked.

"The Virgin Mary...La Madre. You are an amazing woman Laurie Beth. I love watching you, I love how wise you are", he replied.

And there it was, our course was set, I had to see this relationship through the eyes of a 5 year old, I had to see this little girl's world, a world that feels conflicted at times, she likes that Mom and Dad don't fight anymore but she liked the way her family used to be, intact, under one roof. As for me, I just wanted to be Laurie Beth, whatever that was to her. I wasn't thinking about a family, marriage, step-mother status, I am not even divorced yet! I would hope that if or when Andre entered into a relationship, I would want the same for Alec and Ashie, a woman to love my kids, there is no competition for importance, no jockeying for a position or title.

Of course, true to his stripes, Andre had somehow discovered that I was dating Alejandro, our relationship was not a secret, but it certainly was not broadcasted for the obvious reasons. Over the next eight months, Andre would show up at the hospital unexpectedly, pleading with me to take him back, to give him another chance. There is part of me that pitied him, it was as if he had sold his dignity to the devil, kneeling with hands clutched asking for forgiveness. What an interesting concept, this concept of forgiveness. It looks like this, "you wronged me because you didn't do or did do what I don't like, so I am going to hold this experience against you and use it as a weapon to protect myself so that you won't do it again". It is so backwards. It is not me that needed to forgive him, he did what he did and there is not a thought in the world that would or could undo it. I no longer need protection from his acts of alcoholism, prostitution or gambling, that was severed months ago. He is the one who needs to forgive himself for how he wronged himself, and as a result, marital agreements were renegotiated. He never seemed to get it when I would tell him this, in the end, he would just become angry and attacking when he didn't hear what he wanted to hear. I remember so clearly, this one time when he came to the hospital. He appeared on the unit as if he was a magician. I looked at my partner Tricia, she knew my look, startled, annoyed, patient. Tricia is such an awesome partner; she had been a nurse forever, she was a mother hen and I was in her coop. We had this code to extricate me from these impromptu plea bargaining meetings that Andre would hold, she would over-head page me, that was my out. She always knew where I would be when we met, it was just that mother instinct in her, she didn't like the smell of his desperation.

It was an average day at the hospital when I had received an email from the VP of Operations and Staff Services. "A bouquet of flowers was delivered to you here in Administration, from a Dr.

Boo Morales". Are you kidding me? "Boo" is what I call Alejandro? Who did this? Is this a joke? It all became so clear...it was Andre. Once again, an attempt to somehow get back at me, get me in trouble with the hospital, as if having a consenting relationship with another person who works there is illegal, unethical or grounds for termination? Unbelievable. "Thank you but I do not know who this is, but I will come down to get them, I will give them to the volunteers, I am sure there is a patient who needs a smile". Alejandro was not phased, cats meow, dogs bark and sometimes, ex's will be ex's.

We just didn't know how far he would go.

PART THREE

A NEW DREAM

DECISION TREE

*"The greatest part of our happiness or misery depends
on our dispositions and not on our circumstances.*

- Martha Washington

SEPTEMBER 24, 2010. Alejandro and I woke to the doorbell
ringing. 4:08 a.m. Nothing good is behind a doorbell at 4:08
a.m. We looked at each other.

"I'll be right back", as he grabbed the bat under his side of the
bed.

I sat there and rocked back and forth, "I'm not good Alec, I'm
not doing good baby. Please help me, help me". I hear the faint
conversation between Alejandro and a man at the door, "Scottsdale Police, girlfriend, no alarm". Then the door lock and foot-
steps up the stairs.

"That was the Scottsdale police, they said that they received a
distress call from this house. I told him that it was just you and
I sleeping. He asked if we had an alarm system for the house,
but the alarm hasn't been active ever since my ex-wife left", he
explained.

"Alejo, I am not doing good", I said as my eyes welled up.

"What do you mean?".

"Every night, and I mean every night, I dream that Andre is killing me. He is murdering me, with a knife. Just stabbing me over and over. I can't escape, I can't escape this".

"Come here baby", he said pulling me into his chest.

"I want to go home, I just want to go home".

He held me in his arms and stroked my hair until I fell asleep. I guess the decision was made for me. This is unsurvivable. I am so scared of what I have found, I thought that I could do this.

When we woke in the morning, Alejandro called ADT alarm systems and confirmed that the system had not been active and there was no call dispatched to the police last night.

"Do you think it was the boys?", Alejandro said with a tone.

"I know it was. There is no other explanation", I said with a confidently calm tone. Now Alejandro is a scientist by training and a pragmatist by nature. He does not subscribe to supernatural causes, after worlds, miracles or the like. When your body dies, your brain dies and when that happens, there is no "you". That is his philosophy, so to have an inexplicable happening occur is just down right freaky for him. As for me, I knew that it was my boys. They know in what dire straits I am in right now, they know that my spirit wants to be reunited with them, to go there. Home.

Ronnie called me the following day and asked me to come over to his house.

"We need to talk darling, I need to ask you a question Laurie and I'm serious".

There was no fairy dust in that request, no glitter. It was like being called into the principal's office.

"What do you want to know Ronnie?", I asked as I scooped

up Louis. The police had found Louis in Asher's crib, sitting there waiting for him to return as he did many times before, waiting for his baby, waiting for milk. Ronnie and William took Louis to live with William and Ronnie on the day after the boys were killed, my only possession left that meant anything to me.

"I don't like the way you smell, and I'm not talking about your perfume. Now, I want to know, and no one would begrudge you, are you going to kill yourself?".

" Not now", I said matter of factly.

"Well sweetheart, let's talk about this. We need to figure this out or not".

" I don't think we can, I have already been to see 3 counselors, 2 just cried, and the last one who has a doctorate in thanatology just looked at me, cried and said "There's grief and complicated grief and then there's this, and I don't even know what to do with this". I'm a freak, I feel like a freak", I yelled, "No one knows what to do with me, I don't know what to do with me?!".

"Well Laurie, now Laurie, you're my girl and I think I found a way for us to walk out of this".

"You did?".

"There is a woman, her name is Byron Katie. She has walked out of hell herself and has a method of how you and I are going to as well".

"Is she here?".

"No, but I have been reading and practicing what she teaches. We need to find the truth of what happened, of all of this. What happened. Why did it happen? What now? What lies ahead for us? All of it sweetheart. That's the way out. By looking at one belief at a time. But I need for you to stay alive in order to do <u>it</u>. I am OK if you don't want to live baby because I know how much pain you are in, but if that is your decision, then at least let's try one last thing, we have nothing to lose".

"OK Ronnie, I'll try it, that's true, I have nothing to lose".

We just held each other and cried. He knew that I was ready to stop walking, I was disappearing and we both knew that we needed to find a way to bring me back, fast.

GET TO WORK

"Suffering is optional"

- Byron Katie

THE WORK FOUND Byron Katie in 1985 and it found us in 2011. Ronnie and I spent every Saturday, weekend after weekend, month after month, for hours at his house looking at what is, finding the truth of the death of the boys, my future, Andre, finding answers to torturous questions such as "Why didn't I_____? Will I ever feel happy again? Will this pain go away? What happens if I forget Alec and Asher? What is my purpose now? How can I stay safe?" Huge existential thoughts that demanded a truthful answer. I thought we were crazy, after all, our truth was that reality sucked, did we really want to look at this? Have it more in our face? We both knew that we had to give this a try, we both felt my virtual hourglass of time ticking down and just how desperate the situation was becoming, knowing that it was the last attempt to exit Antarctica. And in order to do that, I would have to tackle monumental conceptual mountains in the quest to find truth. Concept 1: What is the truth of my reality? Concept 2: What can I control? Concept 3: What now? What then?

The Work is a simple yet powerful process of inquiry that teaches you to identify and question the thoughts that cause all the suffering in the world. It's a way to understand what's hurting you, and to address the cause of your problems with clarity.

So, here's how it was mapped out to us, our understanding of the teachings of *The Work* and how we used it to walk out of hell. *The Work* directed us to reality, otherwise known as truth, and there are only two kinds of truth: truth is either what is true for us as individuals or truth meaning what is in front of us. My truth as an individual may look like this: Being prompt is a good quality to have, I am funny, Italy is the best country to vacation in, orange is the coolest color. Now this may not be your truth, yours may be: Being on time is overrated, Laurie's not that funny, blue is the best color and France is the best place to vacation. It's not right or wrong, it's just our individual truths. The other type of truth is what is in front of us: reality. It is simply acknowledging what is. That's it. Every belief will be vetted against one of these.

In reality, on this rock called Earth that we live on, there are only 3 types of business: mine, yours and God's. The definitions are simple: my business is everything in myself that I can control, your business is everything in you that is out of my control and God's business is everything that is uncontrollable.

My business may be what I want to put in my body, what is my concept of something that is healthy or unhealthy, risky or not, what excites me, what's my concept of being on time, whether I like you or not, what is good for me.

Your business, other peoples' business, may be what is excites you, how do you want to care for your body, what's your concept of being on time, if you like me or not, what's good for you. We cannot control anyone or anything outside of ourselves, this is law. At first, I balked at this concept, what do you mean we can't control others? Well my theory quickly came to a halt, as it was pointed out to me as I looked around my life, that if I could, Andre would have never killed the children. If we could control other people, children would do everything their parents wanted them to do and vice versa; there would be no need for marriage counseling, or recidivism in the prison system. Now, what we can do is attempt to influence and manipulate others, to get them to think, feel, behave or have a story that we want them to have about us. However, once we take away the influence, people are going to think, feel and behave the way they want to and I can't change that. You may relate to it this way, I can put on a particular uniform or article of clothing, wear makeup or tell you stories about myself (or not!), I can bully or threaten you, give you rewards or compliments, or even punish you in an attempt to get you to perceive, feel or interact with me the way I want you to. But when I remove all of that, when my spell has worn off, you are going to think, feel and interact with me the way YOU want to, and I cannot control that.

And lastly, God's business, otherwise known as reality. Now, I am not referring to a religious leader, God = Reality and Reality is God because it rules every time, and the definition is everything that is out of my control, your control and anyone's control. Such examples are floods, people being born, death, war, falling in love, lying. There is not a person in the world who has been able to control any of these.

Putting this all together, when we have a thought that, in an instant, takes us out of our own business, meaning what we can control, the result is separation, we are separate from ourselves, from what we can control. We find ourselves in a place trying to control someone or something that we can't, resulting in feelings of anger, anxiety, frustration and sadness; simply put, we are wild, out of control, literally. It is insanity, simply because it is insane to attempt to control something that you can't, we actually call that mental illness on some definitive level. We feel alone and resentful. This premise of "who's business are you in" helps to initially guide us to where we are when we begin to investigate or vet our beliefs that we are serving. Whenever I am in your business, demanding how you should be, what is right/wrong, good/bad, moral/immoral, or in God's business, pushing aside what is in front of me and arrogantly demanding how this place is/isn't supposed to run, I will always find myself hopelessly at war, only to be defeated 100% of the time. We have thoughts like this all the time, "you should lose weight, people shouldn't be so judgmental, people should be kinder". I love what Katie teaches in regards to this concept of who's business we are in,"...it is arrogant, even in the name of love, for me to think I know what is best for you, I just know what is best for me".

In its most basic form, *The Work* consists of four simple questions and the turnarounds:

1. Is it true? (Yes or no. If no, move to 3.)

2. Can you absolutely know that it's true? (Yes or no.)

3. How do you react, what happens, when you believe that thought?

4. Who would you be without the thought?

Turn around: (to self, to the other, to the opposite)

It sounds really simple but it's not, it's work. As humans, we believe most everything that our mind proposes to us and treats it as if it's true. It is just trying to help us in an attempt to help us interpret what all of this means. But just because we think it, doesn't mean it is true, maybe we once believed in the Tooth Fairy or Santa Claus? Not true. Or at one time, all of us who inhabited the Earth believed that it was flat? Not true. We weren't mentally ill or insane, it was just what we believed, based on our best thinking and what our perceptions told us. I also have learned through Katie that just because something is either true or untrue, does not mean that I like it, condone it or am irreverent to it, it just means that not a thought in the world is going to change it. I am not going to like everything that I experience or don't experience, and that's OK, but if I argue with a reality, rejecting it, posture war with it, as a result of believing a thought that is not true, meaning true for me as an individual or true meaning based in reality, then I will suffer.

So, I am ready, I want to know the truth. The truth of the boys' death. The truth of my future. The truth of my crime, how I could have prevented or stopped it. The truth of my part. It may be true, that I somehow am responsible for the death of my kids, but I need to know for sure. If I am going to convict myself of somehow being culpable for the death of Alec and Asher and in turn, sentence myself to a life of guilt, self-loathing, shame, torture and eventually, death, I better know that it is 100% true. In order to do this, it requires me to set aside right from wrong, good from bad, moral, immoral, fair, unfair. Truth, meaning reality, this little part of the universe that we inhabit doesn't care about this, it just stands neutrally and shows what is. After I finished completing a *Judge Your Neighbor* worksheet, which is a tool of *The Work* in identifying beliefs, Ronnie wrote on a piece of paper in bolded letter, the crime that I had committed, there it was. We both knew that this was the big one, the master belief that had the power to take my life. So the gigs up, there it is right in front of me, in black and white, there was no hiding from it:

BELIEF: As a Mom, it was my job to protect Alec and Asher and I didn't. If I had done things differently, they would be alive. I should have known, I failed them.

Ronnie: 1. Is it true?

Me: YES., I said with an irritated tone, as if I am a teen once again, seeming to answer a stupidly, obvious question. As a Mom, I am supposed to protect my kids, any parent or even people who aren't parents would agree with me.

Ronnie: What's the reality?

Me: The reality is that I didn't protect them.

Ronnie: OK, let's go deeper, why not? What was the thought? Were you just so neglectful and all that you wanted to do was be with Alejandro? Or did you know something and just didn't do anything about it? Why Laurie, why didn't you know? You see this belief screams, "You are somehow responsible for the death of the children".

Me: Because I didn't know that Andre was dangerous. I didn't know that anyone could do such a thing. I didn't believe that they were in danger dammit, I can't predict the future? (wiping the tears form my eyes).

Ronnie: So mothers should be able to detect danger and know when their kids are in danger? Is that true?

Me: No. That's absurd, I couldn't. I can't. I don't know what is going to happen in the next 30 seconds, no one does. I could guess based on what I know, but that's about it.

Ronnie: That's right darling, it's not true. This belief says, "you should have known". No one can predict the future. Based on your theory, children would never be harmed because their mothers would be able to predict and prevent the injury. OK, so we don't need to go to question #2 (Can I be absolutely sure that this belief is true?) because we already answered NO. Let's go to Question #3: How do you react when you think this thought?

Me: It wrecks me, it makes me feel hopeless, helpless, very angry, hostile, resentful, terrified, horrified, victimized, depressed, empty, frustrated, vindictive, bitter, agitated. It makes me push everyone and everything away. It makes me obsess about Andre, it brings me back to the crime scene, it makes my thinking like his, consumed with murderous thoughts of harm. Stuck. Crazy. It makes me doubled-over and howl from the bowels of my soul. It makes me wish that my heart would stop beating when I go to sleep at night, it makes me want to die. It makes me believe that I deserve to die.

Ronnie: Good honey, Katie would say, WELCOME TO HELL. Now how would it feel, what would you have left if you couldn't think this thought?

Me: Oh, that's hard. (Long pause of silence) Relieved. No guilt. I would still feel really sad because I don't have my boys, but I wouldn't be punishing myself, I wouldn't want to kill myself.

Ronnie: Wow, that is amazing, so we see that it may not be the boys' death that is torturing you, it is this belief, a belief that is not true. And I don't know about you, but we will take less suffering, less depression, less torture any day!

Me: (Smiling with tears) I agree.

My theory is starting to fall apart.

Ronnie: OK darling, now for the turn-around...

Me: I couldn't have protected them.

Ronnie: Good, another one.

Me: Sometimes, parents can't protect their kids.

Ronnie: If there's two, there has to be three...

Me: Sometimes there is danger in   places that we are not able to detect, I did not know that Andre was dangerous. He loved Alec and Asher, he never, ever was physically or emotionally abusive to them, I didn't know that he was planning this.

Ronnie: Honey, Andre wasn't dangerous, it was his thinking that was dangerous. Andre just followed his thoughts and you and I are learning that an uninvestigated thought that is acted on can be really dangerous. Go on...

Me: It is my job to protect myself, and what is murdering me right now and a threat of ending my life is a thought. This thought, that I am somehow responsible for the death of my kids. When I believe this thought, I am murdering myself by accepting responsibility for a crime that I did not commit, an impossible catch 22, to predict the future, to know what others are thinking, to identify danger. I don't have this super power, that is insane. It's hopeless.

Ronnie: Keep going...

Me: No one can predict the future, to believe that, "I should have known" is insane. That is the same as me believing," I should have known he was going to murder them". The truth is, I would and could never have thought that thought prior to March 31, 2010. How could I have? If I had made a list of the top

50 things that Andre was capable of or would do to hurt me, murdering the kids was not on the list, ever.

Ronnie: Yes, and isn't the truth that if you did know that he was having murderous thoughts or a plan, you would have done something, anything? We would have taken the kids to Paris, or you would have taken the bullet? If staying married would have kept the boys alive, then I know that you would have never asked for a divorce if that was the trade! You would have done anything to save them if you would have known. Go deeper, even if you didn't get a divorce, took the bullet or absconded with the kids, can we be absolutely sure that he wouldn't have killed them or you? Or that we wouldn't be found by the authorities and sent to jail for kidnapping and he then kill them? Or how about taking the bullet but maybe not die but be a vegetable or severely wounded and couldn't care for the boys and he's in prison? How would Alec and

Asher be then? Happy? Free? And worse, they would have to witness your death?

Me: You are so right, we could go on and on, swirling into stories of what ifs and if onlys and that is torture in and of itself. The reality is, truth, is that I could not have known, I did not know, and if I did, I still would not have been able to protect my kids or myself. We all just can do the best we can and do the next best thing that comes to us when a situation arises. There is no such thing as protection from others or the world, it is all none of my business, it's all out of my control.

Ronnie: I see one more turn around...

Me: It is my job to love Alec and Asher and to do the best that I can as a parent.

Ronnie: Laurie, did you do the best that you could for those babies? Loving them,   watching Andre, hanging in there for 18 months of couples counseling, affairs, alcoholism, and even in the last moment that you saw them?

Me: Yes, I did. The last thing I said to Alec when I put him in Andre's car when Andre was berating screaming at me in the middle of the Jamba Juice parking lot was to whisper in his ear, "I love you Mumsie, you just have buckets of fun with Daddy and Asher, and don't worry, Daddy is just having a tough time right now".

Ronnie: That's right. That's the truth. He was safe, they were safe and you didn't know. You did your job.

Me: (With tears of relief and joy)And here's the biggest truth, Andre is 100% responsible for the death of Alec and Asher. It was his thought and his action. I am in no way responsible for Andre or anyone else's thoughts, feelings or actions. I am in no way responsible for the death of Alec and Asher.

Ronnie: That's true. 100%.

Ronnie just hugged me and whispered in my ear, "It's OK Mom, it's OK", just like Alec used to tell me.

In the process of seeking what I thought would kill me, something has actually been born inside of me. I am on my path, a path where inquiry is alive in me and cannot be extinguished. I would find myself walking towards a new life, a different life, because living the life that I lived before is impossible, it is no longer and trying to would only bring pain. One day, a small package showed up in my mailbox, to my surprise, it was a little statue of a kangaroo with a note:

Laurie Beth,

It is impossible for kangaroos to go backwards, they can only move in 2 directions: forward or in a circle. Just like their beautifully, strong tails behind them, what is behind you will propel your direction. I know that you will choose wisely.

Love, Dad

Humans cannot turn our heads around all the way, it would actually kill us if we did, cutting off our lives instantaneously. Metaphorically, I know now that this is how I need to live. When I attempt to live backwards, I end up in the past, cutting off all life, I die and so does my ability to create a future, after all, how can I look at the direction I am pointed in.

Over the next years, I would be on a journey of discovery, traveling millions of miles as a truth seeker on a quest to return home, the only interference that could sway me off my path is an uninvestigated belief that would propel me in a circular direction, backwards. I had to look at all of them, one by one, and once I found home, it was my job to continue to clean up the space that I live in, my mind. It seemed like an overwhelmingly, tall order, but I found that there were not that many stories, and certainly not that original, just recycled themes with different characters, content and details. I have been asked by many, how did I do it? How did I manage to exit Antarctica? I often ask myself this overwhelming question, but the answer is always the same... Look at what is. Face forward. Keep walking. Be gentle and patient. Keep going deeper. Don't take myself so seriously. Remember that I am not my thinking. Don't settle for anything other than truth.

Here is some of my Work that I humbly share with you about the story of the death of Alec and Ashie. Please notice my vernacular, this is only one belief that comprises the story of the death of my children but it is not the story of them, as they are not defined by a crime, another's actions, or their death, but by their life presence.

BELIEF: Andre wasn't supposed to kill the children.

1. True? Yes. Yes, and Yes.

Of course it's true?! Parents aren't supposed to harm their kids, needless to say, kill them. Aren't parents supposed to protect their kids? They aren't supposed to harm them? Intentionally murder them? What's the reality of it: meaning what is in front of me? The reality is that he did. He killed them. That's right, he did. You see, nothing in reality, in this universe, has ever happened or comes about because it shouldn't have. Now, we may not like it, expect it, approve of it, or want it, but there are no mistakes. Truth is what is in front of us. Example: I have green eyes. How do I know that is true? Because I do, if I wasn't supposed to have green eyes, I wouldn't have them. Example: People are supposed to die. That is true, how do we know that: because they do, all living things do, they are supposed to. Now this question is not asking, "Do I like that the boys died, did the boys deserve to die, was it right what Andre did", this question is just gently bringing me into reality. OK, so it's not true. The truth is that he did,

2. Can I be absolutely sure that this thought is true? NO. I don't even need to go here because it's already been proven that he was supposed to because his thought dictated his behavior.

3. How do I react when I think this thought? Hopeless, helpless, angry, hostile, resentful, terrified, horrified, victimized, depressed, empty, frustrated, vindictive, bitter, agitated. It makes me push everyone and everything away. It makes me obsess about Andre, it brings me back to the crime scene, it makes my thinking like his, consumed with murderous thoughts of harm. Stuck. Crazy. As Katie would say, WELCOME TO HELL.

4. Who would I be without the thought? Less. Less all of that in #3. I actually would be able to comprehend, not condone but understand what Byron Katie is teaching when she says, "an un-investigated thought isn't dangerous unless we believe it".

Think of a recurring stressful situation, a situation that is reliably stressful even though it may have happened only once in your mind. As you answer each of the questions below, allow yourself to mentally revisit the time and place of the stressful occurrence. Use short, simple sentences.

In this situation, who angers, confuses, saddens, or disappoints you, and why?
I am *furious, disgusted* with _Andre_ because he killed the children, he betrayed their trust with the intent to hurt & punish me. He destroyed everyone's lives —
Example: I am angry with Paul because he doesn't listen to me.

In this situation, how do you want them to change? What do you want them to do?
I want _Andre_ to burn in hell. I want him to be tortured for the rest of his life. I want him to die. I want him to spend every waking moment conscious that he killed the children. I want him to never feel love again.
Example: I want Paul to see that he is wrong. I want him to stop lying to me. I want him to see that he is killing himself.

In this situation, what advice would you offer to them?
Andre should/shouldn't shouldn't have been so vindictive, angry, juvenile, and a bully. Andre should have had the balls to accept responsibility for his actions of fucking 27 models & been humble in getting a divorce. Andre should have gotten therapy & help. You should have killed me. He should have protected them. He should have killed himself & him
Example: Paul should take a deep breath. He should calm down. He should see that his behavior frightens me. He should know that being right is not worth another heart attack.

In order for you to be happy in this situation, what do you need them to think, say, feel, or do?
I need _Andre_ to do nothing except remain incarcerated. I need nothing from him because nothing can bring back my kids. I don't fucking care what happens to that piece of shit called Andre.
Example: I need Paul to hear me when I talk to him. I need him to take care of himself. I need him to admit that I am right.

What do you think of them in this situation? Make a list. (Remember, be petty and judgmental.)
Andre is petty, immature, vindictive, evil, dangerous, spiteful, stupid a coward.
Example: Paul is unfair, arrogant, loud, dishonest, way out of line, and unconscious.

What is it about this situation that you don't ever want to experience again?
I don't ever want to experience the death of my children again.

Example: I don't ever want Paul to lie to me again. I don't ever want to see him ruining his health again.

Now investigate each of the above statements using the four questions. Always give yourself time to let the deeper answers meet the questions. Then turn each thought around. For the turnaround to statement 6, replace the words "I don't ever want to..." with "I am willing to..." and "I look forward to..." Until you can look forward to all aspects of life without fear, your Work is not done.

The four questions
Example: Paul doesn't listen to me.
1. Is it true? (Yes or no. If no, move to 3.)
2. Can you absolutely know that it's true? (Yes or no.)
3. How do you react, what happens, when you believe that thought?
4. Who would you be without the thought?

Turn the thought around
a) to the self. (I don't listen to myself.)
b) to the other. (I don't listen to Paul.)
c) to the opposite. (Paul does listen to me.)
Then find at least three specific, genuine examples of how each turnaround is true for you in this situation.

My "Judge Your Neighbor Worksheet"
by The Work

Andre had a thought, just like I do, like we all do. He believed it, with no tools to vet it, and then acted upon it. Just like I would be doing if I acted on the belief, "Killing myself will put me out of pain", "My life is over, I have nothing if I don't have my children" or " I can't live here without my kids, I will never be happy again so what's the point".

Turn arounds:

1. The kids were killed. If I take it a step further, Andre was supposed to do this because he believed a thought, something probably like this," If I kill the boys, it'll destroy Laurie", " I'll show her what she did to our family", or " if I can't get what I want, then no one will", or maybe," I'll show her who gets the last word". Who knows what he was thinking. Now I know, being in the mental health field for 20+ years, if one wants to know why we do what we do, it is a simple algorithm: everything, and I mean everything, that has been created or destroyed by man, began with a thought, thoughts produce feelings and thoughts plus feelings lead to behaviors. That is law. Based on Andre's best thinking at the time, which was "I'll kill the children and then myself", I can begin to understand how he arrived at his deadly deed.

2. Sometimes children are killed by their parents. Sometimes children kill their parents. Sometimes we kill ourselves. We don't get to pick and choose how long we live, none of us do. Even people who kill themselves believe that they no longer have a choice to live.

3. I am killing the kids. When I have this belief, I am having an infatuation with death, with a crime and I can't see them, I can't access my kids, I can't connect with them. I can't see them playing trains, eating ice cream, snuggling with Cow Cow. I just see a crime scene. I am in the story of injustice and victimization.

4. I am killing me. Look at what this belief does to me; it is murdering me, it is killing all life, love and happiness that lives inside of me. By believing these thoughts and arguing with reality, I will only be destroyed, psychologically, emotionally and then eventually, physically. And if I die, they die. Alec and Ashie live inside of me, if I die, they die. If I die, who will be the one to share with others, just how great my boys are?

5. The kids are not dead. As Steve resonates to me from A Course In Miracles, "Nothing is so blinding as perception of form, and perception is the story we are telling ourselves about what we see with our eyes. And it reinforces the belief that we are only a body, once the body is gone, we are gone". This is just not true, because none of us live our lives in front of each other all of the time, and we don't go into mental distress. Truth is, is that we can feel connected with anyone and dream with anyone, spirit to spirit through the mind, not needing a body to be present. We dream about others and the future all the time, and it feels so real. We do this when we are pregnant and fantasize about what the baby will look like, when we leave an awesome first date, when we are thinking about a new career opportunity. We don't need anything or anyone in front of us to feel happy, the minute we believe this, it is hopelessly painful. Now I get it, when Byron Katie says, "In my life, no one is powerful enough to leave me". Now I get it, they are alive in me, only I can make them disappear. They live in my mind, and it is impossible for them to ever leave me, how could they, they are my children.

So, I have my work cut out for me. Truth is inside of me and I am determined to find it, one belief at a time. I am aware that these beliefs are like an ant's nest, only to see the surface yet a colony of supporting thoughts lay below. I will not be afraid of these thoughts, they are just thoughts. Some are master beliefs that seem humungous and truth seems to be unobtainable, but I have and will continue to find the truth to everything and will not rest until these beliefs no longer have power over me. Even if I still believe only 1% of the thought, it is still alive and has power over me, it will still cause suffering. It is equal to an invisible, malignant, cancer cell, just one has the power to cause destruction. Here are the many beliefs that I have found the truth of over the past seven years. This is not a one-shot exercise, I have deconstructed the story which is comprised of these beliefs numerous times until one by one, they lost their power.

Belief: I should have known (Master belief).

Belief: I am somehow responsible for the death of my kids (Master belief).

Belief: I will never be happy again (Master belief).

Belief: He disrespected me.

Belief: The kids died alone.

Belief: The kids were aware that they were being killed.

Belief: The kids were in pain.

Belief: Alec and Asher shouldn't have died. They died too soon.

Belief: If I am happy or create a life, it means that I am OK with their death.

Belief: I am afraid that I will forget about Alec and Asher.

Belief: Everyone has forgotten about them/what happened.

Belief: He deserves to die.

Belief: I can't love you as much as Alec and Asher.

Belief: I need to remind you of Alec and Asher and what happened.

Belief: God is cruel and mean.

Belief: I wish that I would have died instead.

Belief: I want them back.

Belief: I wish that Alec and Asher were alive.

Belief: I miss them.

Belief: Alec and Asher are gone.

Belief: How come everyone else gets to get a divorce and I don't?

Belief: Why me?

Belief: I can't handle this.

Belief: Alec and Asher would have had a great life, they were robbed.

Belief: It's not fair.

Belief: I'll never be a mother again. I am not a Mom.

Belief: I will always hurt.

Belief: He took my happiness.

So, I have chosen to find truth, but what of it? Does that mean that I am choosing life? Does this mean that I need to stay here now? But I had a plan, to leave once the trial was over. Could it be even possible that I may not want to leave now? *Is* it possible to be here, even without Alec and Asher and be happy? Is it possible that I could or would survive the death of my children?

Who knows what the future holds, but the past says that I did survive the death of Alec and Asher and I guess right now, in this moment, I am alive, adapting and I can live with that.

MI FAMILIA NUEVA

"Come to the edge", he said.

They said, "We are afraid".

"Come to the edge", she said again.

They came.

She pushed them.

And they flew...

I'LL NEVER FORGET HOW he proposed to me. It was about a year and a half after the boys died, I was in bed reading a book on the Holocaust, (just some light reading before bed), waiting for my Boo to come home from playing squash with the boys. At that time, I was fascinated with books related to the Holocaust, on a very basic level, I found this strange but comforting kindred connection with them; one moment you are living your life, the next your family is murdered and you are the only survivor. The place that you thought was safe, felt as if it betrayed you. It wasn't just the tragedy that resonated with me, the fear of the earth opening up again and swallowing me up with it, but it was the relentless drive to continue to live, to make myself such that I can tolerate anything, to be impervious to suffering. I had to remind myself

My honey and me

that we can only see a certain distance in front of us, beyond that, we will need to trust and let go.

"Beth" (that's what Alejandro calls me), Alejandro kneeled at my bedside. "I want to talk to you. You know, I wanted *us*, all 6 of us, but we didn't get that. But you gave me my girls back, you gave me a family, you make my life better. I love my life and I love you. So would you marry me?". Now the only thing that could have made this more romantic is if he said it in Spanish.

I was taken aback, was I ready to be married again? What would this mean? Is it OK to get married after the boys died? The answers just naturally came from within, of course, I am, I already am married to him and the girls. As for Alec and Asher, it was clear that my grief was independent of my love for my life and those in it. There are no timelines for *when*, as if waiting is somehow a reflection of how much I hurt or love? Measuring time does not work and neither does waiting to live again.

"I know how much you love me and how we dreamed of the 6 of us", I said as I gently admired his Virgin Mary charm on his necklace in between my fingers. "I have traveled a million miles to make it back home and you never grew tired of waiting for me, you always kept the light on. I would love to marry you and we will marry when I can marry all of you, when I have three proposals. So I accept and until then, patiently wait knowing that I claim you and you me". "I love you woman, I love how much you love my girls", he quietly whispered in my ear. "Well, the Virgin Mary is divine, she knew exactly what a good Catholic boy needed…a nice, Jewish girl.".

God that feels so long ago and then not so distant. I felt so innocent, so naive when I think of that time. My vocabulary to describe my life was different; words such as murder, cremation, trial were nonexistent except when watching an episode of *Law and Order*, now I was living it. We somehow were morphing into a family; routines were easier, moments of happiness were more frequent and I found myself less often in Antarctica. I was still in a great deal of pain, but I don't know if I will ever be pain free, it just becomes less intense, less frequent. One day, I was jogging with Adele and Juliet, a common routine that I acquired after the death of the boys. Running for me was metaphorical for how I have to live my life, just one foot in front of the next, it doesn't matter how fast or where you are going, just keep moving. And just when you think that there is no way in the world you can keep going, you do, farther than you ever imaged.

Adele: "Laurie, can we ask you something?"

Me: (Thinking to myself, "Oh gosh, I hope this isn't something big because I can barely breathe needless to say talk and run") "Sure."

Adele: "Well, do you remember when we first met and I told you that you weren't my Mom and then Alec said that Ashie and he were lucky to have you as a Mom? "

Me: "Yes."

Adele: "Well, you made Daddy happy again, My Dad and my Mom were not happy together, they fought a lot and I hated that. I was scared because I thought

that I would never have a family like some other kids. So, we'd like to know if we could be the lucky ones and have you as our Step-mom?"

I stopped.

Juliet: "Laurie, what Adele is trying to say is that we all talked it over as a family and we want to know if you will marry us?"

There are no words to say. No words to describe. No script. This is us. We just hugged each other in the middle of the street, I could have stayed there forever. I can't believe it, I have no idea how this all came together, my best planning would not have given me such a beautiful family, at least I didn't believe so. It has been an unbelievable whirlwind, being on the highest high, to the lowest low and now, actually allowing myself to love again and allowing others to love me. An absolute miracle.

Juliet: "Dad! She said yes! We are getting married!" (running into the house)

Adele: "We all should wear white with orange", Adele said with an excited smile.

Juliet: "Not all of us, I want to wear yellow because that was Ashie's favorite color, yellow".

Alejandro: "Orange and yellow it is! "

Laurie: "We are getting married!"

We were married on September 17th, the four of us, my Mom and Dad, Ronnie and William. Everyone said their vows to each other, it was a true commitment ceremony, an expression of love for each other and a shared dream that we all have, as individuals and as a family. When it came to my Mom sharing her thoughts, she pulled out an essay that I had written in tenth grade, titled "My American Dream". I wouldn't have believed it if I didn't see it with my own eyes, but in my essay, my American dream stated:

Our wedding day: Juliet, Me, Alejandro and Adele

"...*my dream that means the most to me is to fall in love with a rich, good-looking, Spanish man who will keep me happy for the rest of my life. In the future, I really hope that my dreams turn into reality. In contrast, if my dreams were to slowly disappear one by one, I would still be happy because I love the life I have and I am glad to live in my country, America.*".

Now that is unbelievable, a call of fate memorialized 25 years ago from the past.

Our story is simple, it is a love story. Now, I'm not wild about some Disney storylines but maybe dreams do come true...a prince, a princess, a fairy Godmother?

The men of my life: William, Daddy, Alejandro and Ronnie

Following our small ceremony of the eight of us (plus Steve who officiated), went to Maestro's City Hall, one of our favorite restaurants, no pun intended. Every year we go there to celebrate our matrimony as a family.

I was in. 100%. I no longer see me disappearing; death was no longer an option, I want to live. And live happy. If I am going to be here, then I am going to be here living happy, or else what's the point? To live here and suffer? Not any more, not that way. I remember what my Dad told me, "Do not make anyone or

Mi Familia Nueva: 2011

anything so powerful as to make you feel happy or unhappy". I despise Andre and his crime, but I will not give my power away to dictate the condition that I live here by. So, thank you, Oneness, whoever or whatever you are. Every past experience has prepared me to live this very moment.

Thank you, I have a family. Again.

THE OTHER EX-

*Three things in human life are important, the
first is to be kind, the second is to be kind, the
third is to be kind.*

- Mother Teresa

LIFE FOR OUR FAMILY was so natural, we were like a "normal"
family: parent pick-up after school followed by homework,
dinnertime discussions about the "highs and lows" of our day,
playing a game, Apples to Apples or Uno are our favs, and then
bedtime. Bedtime is always my favorite, it is the period at the
end of the sentence. The gift that we have as parents to teach our
kids that their work for the day is over; it is a time to let go and
reflect on all the bounty that came to you today. After we said
our reflections on the day and whispers of love, I would sing a
song to Adele and Juliet, just like I did with Alec and Ashie, but
differently. It wasn't Elton John, it wasn't smelling their hair, that
was a specific ritual that could not be replicated, at least for now.
Believe it or not, it was karaoke. We bought Adele a microphone
for her 7th birthday, as she has a love for singing, so each night
the girls would take turns choosing a song for me to sing to them
while they drifted off.

That's not to say that I didn't continue to have my moments, or several, where the feeling of continual sadness lingered, but it no longer gripped me into the depths of hell, and if it did, I visited Antarctica less often and I didn't stay there as long. Unbeknownst to us, while we went about our routines, there was an all too familiar agenda being born from his ex-wife, to take the kids away from Alejandro.

The best way to describe Alejandro's ex-wife from my perception and from what I have been told from other's who once befriended her, is that she is a very angry bird. We have attempted to theorize about the sources of her anger from what Alejandro has shared, but no one except his ex really knows, and it's possible that she may not even know. From what I have been told, when they met, Alejandro had been in Boston for about a year. He was learning our American ways and mastering his fluency in English; he saw her as a great advocate that helped him navigate through the Ivy League system, residency and fellowship placements and she was a potential suitor for motherhood. In her mind, she deserved payback in the form of compliance, he owed her. She wanted him to be a Harvard professor, wearing Brooks Brothers shirts and living as an academic. Skiing in Vermont, vacationing only with her parents and quietly nodding his head to her every request, those which included dictated activities with the children as she saw fit, limiting his soccer and squash games and distancing himself from his roots in Colombia. Their marriage lasted about 11 years, with the relationship unraveling in its infancy.

When Alejandro and I were dating about 3 months, she requested that he leave his thriving practice in Scottsdale to return with her to Boston which he declined for obvious reasons. She was stuck in Arizona. According to Alejandro, this infuriated her, he describes her response similar to a petulant child whose parents gave her everything. Then there was me, I embodied every quality that she detested; skinny, wore make up, nails painted, you know, "one of those girls". But she didn't even know me, I was a book judged by my cover. It didn't matter if I graduated college cum-laude, came from a respectable Jewish family (she is Jewish too), and most of all, loved her kids. Regardless of the reason, she was a wet hen and prided herself at mastering the sport of lawyering up and taking Alejandro to Court if she didn't get her way. Juliet was too young to see this but Adele understood glimmers of her mother's dislike for her father and her contemptuous disposition for the divorce decree.

Our relationship with her, or should I say mine, wasn't always adversarial, I didn't have anything against her and I couldn't imagine her having anything against me. I was not the other woman, I met Alejandro well after their divorce. If anything, one would have thought I met the most important criteria, I loved her kids. In the beginning, our relationship was civil, we attended Adele and Juliet's horse shows together, exchanged recipes and celebrated birthdays together. It was great, families coming together with a common ground, to love these two girls. But the dynamic changed the minute that my boys had died.

II finally grasped the depths of her disregard for me, as there are only 3 people on this earth who knew me who didn't not offer condolences or support to Alejandro and me after the boys were killed, not an "I'm so sorry" or "what can I do to help", a hug, nothing. And when I mean nothing, I mean nothing ; Andre, Andre's mother Jeannette (the boys' grandmother) and Alejandro's ex-wife. I will refrain from further comment, as this speaks for itself. Something that she wrote in an email to Alejandro shortly after Alec and Asher died, one of the many for the following years to come, still resonates with us: "I am concerned and caution you that Laurie is trying to replace her boys by trying to be Adele and Juliet's mother. She can participate as an adult in their lives but Adele and Juliet have a mother". All of a sudden, I was perceived by her as a threat, not a woman who loved her children, but an adversary under some crazed theory that I was using Juliet and Adele to somehow replace Alec and Asher (which is impossible) or take her children away from her (also impossible and unthinkable), and that my relationship with the girls had anything to do with her. She would come to our door to pick them up or drop off clothes and she would say nothing. I could understand even when people would say, "I don't know what to say", I could get that, but nothing, no acknowledgment? I still to this day cannot relate how anyone can lack such compassion towards someone who's children were killed.

His ex waged her first attack in August, 2010 when she decided to appoint herself as the judge in presiding over their divorce decree. At the time of their separation and finalization of the divorce decree, parenting time was about 35/65 and very one-sided. Alejandro forfeited some of his parenting time for the needs of the kids, Adele had just turned 4 and Juliet was still a toddler in the midst of being potty trained, and with his soon to be ex-wife being only a part-time physician, it just made sense. Alejandro had no Thanksgivings, no Father's Day, and limited vacations with the kids in addition to the skeleton regular school year schedule so every day that he was with his girls was precious. It is understandable then, that when she precipitously decided to take back the following day she had given Alejandro to spend with the girls, he declined. Like a petulant child being denied a second scoop of ice cream, friend no more, she threatened to call the police and charge him with violating their custody agreement. It didn't matter that he had plans to take them to Disney On Ice or that the kids were sleeping, his attempts to reason with her fell on deaf ears. Fifteen minutes after her demand, Alejandro received a telephone call from the Scottsdale police. Unbelievable. It was 8:30 p.m. on Sunday night, and she wanted us to wake up the kids and drive them 24 miles (one way) to her house because she "changed her mind". Alejandro offered to acquiesce, as he was not going to subject the children to this nor was he willing to risk his getting tied up in a legal battle of defending fabricated allegations. The police somehow managed to convince his ex to back down for the wellness of the children, but it was clear what we needed to do.

June, 2012, six months later, which is a short amount of time given the love of attorneys to file motions to the motions and her arbitrary nature, the divorce decree was revised in a Rule 69 Agreement. Alejandro had regained his parenting time, all of it, vacation time and holidays were shared and reciprocated equally. But of course, this only incensed her.

Now there are a few dates that stick in my mind, fortunately or unfortunately, and August 8, 2012 is one of them, Juliet came home from school upset, stating, "I was sent to the front office to talk to this woman who was in my private business, asking me if I was happy with my family and if I feel scared at home or if anyone in my family has ever hurt me". My social worker ears perked up, I was too familiar with this routine from my days as a clinical director of Maricopa County children services. CPS had been called. But by who? School had just begun 1 day ago. In disbelief, Alejandro and I rushed to meet with the school principal to inquire what this was all about, only to verify from the school safety officer that the school had not made any report, it was an outside source. When Alejandro called his ex-wife to ask if she had known that Juliet had been interviewed and that CPS had been called, she calmly confirmed that she knew about the meeting but denied that it was her. Such an unusual response by a parent whose kids are allegedly being harmed. Why didn't she call Alejandro? And if an "outsider" had any concerns of abuse, they would have called both parents to investigate? Why hadn't she received that same phone call from CPS to meet with her? It was becoming clearer, his ex-wife was the reporter, she had called CPS on us, but we would need confirmation with such an accusation.

The following days waiting to meet with CPS were horrible, filled with anxiety and anticipation. It reminds me of when you hear the other "C" word, you know, Cancer. Cancer = Death, CPS = you're are going to have your kids taken away from you. Not again. Now Adele and Juliet? On the outside, I was fearless but on the inside I was terrified, I can't lose 2 more children. We had nothing to hide; when Alejandro received the phone call from Lauren Y., CPS investigator, we gladly invited her in to any aspect of our home and lives. After she toured our home, the three of us sat at the kitchen table as she read the allegations: It is reported that Dad throws Adele and Juliet against the walls when she does not do her homework and he is physically assaultive towards his wife. Me? The man who has stood by my side in my darkest time? The man who said his only regret in life is that he didn't hold Alec on behalf of me until the coroner's office showed up? The man who calls his girls "my beautiful moñequas" (which means dolls in Spanish)? Alejandro is a spicy, Latin male and makes it clear that he is their Daddy and not their friend, he may raise his voice and scream "Carajo!" when he gets frustrated but child abuse? And what about me? I have paid the ultimate price as a result of child abuse, a parent killing their children. I love Adele and Juliet and would protect them with my life, as I would have if I could have with Alec and Asher if I knew of one's plan to harm them. I would never let anyone harm them. After an hour of being peppered with numerous questions, she had reached her conclusion: *Findings: unfounded and inconclusive, case closed".* We eventually obtained the report through our lawyer and there it was, in black and white, 3rd sentence in. She eventually copped to it, but true to her nature, she blamed him.

We breathed a sigh of relief, but what now? What next? We had another wolf in a sheep costume. No, that's not accurate, there isn't even a bother with the sheep costume, we had a scorpion on our hands.

The harassment did not stop there. For the next year, Alejandro and I were the recipients of copious hate emails, accusations of not feeding the girls nutritious lunches, sending them to school tired, or not supporting Adele playing cello because we had also purchased her a violin and a flute. Crazy demands such as taking Adele to get her passport picture and renewal and then when we did, she ripped up the picture in front of Adele, emailing that, "she had to retake the picture because she looks like a hoochie". You would have thought that it was a one-time occurrence, a fluke, once, but the identical situation appeared again when it was Juliet's turn. Juliet was so excited to get her passport picture, she came downstairs with beautiful braids, "I think I am going to look so pretty for my passport book", she said, only to have that photo discarded. When Alejandro confronted his ex about how deflated Juliet felt and the ridiculousness of running around to get photos just to have them thrown away, the response was, "what's the big deal, so we will take another picture". What's the big deal? What?! This is an ugly aspect of some divorces, the fighting doesn't stop. Isn't that why people get divorced in the first place? Anyways, the girls were watching and sometimes what your kids witness is unpreventable, but when they look at their passport book today, we just stay focused on their numerous stamps from all of the great places they have traveled.

The attacks escalated to a whole different level, they became physical. Alejandro shared that she had a history of kicking him when they were married, but would never think of me being a target. A funny thing happens to a person after they know that someone had a plan to murder them, it just makes every other threat seem less than. As for me, I can hold my own, after all, not too long ago I had a bullet waiting for me, so having a heavy set, Jewish woman lunge or strike me was nothing. Another funny thing happens to you once your kids are murdered, you get a lot of legal support, from everywhere. My life no longer was private and neither were the lives of those who were related or "close to me". The prosecutors, district attorney, private investigators and police left no stone unturned, no legal history unread, everyone was investigated and as a victim they wanted to make sure that I felt safe. Shockingly, I had found out that his ex and her parents had restraining orders against them from one of their neighbors. One side of my brain was in disbelief because I was raised in a non-violent, non-physical home so waging an attack on someone is completely foreign. On the other hand, I could believe it, not just because of her disposition towards us but because I no longer held the belief ,"oh, they wouldn't do that, that couldn't happen". That belief disintegrated the moment I found out what Andre had done.

It was Spring, 2012 and Juliet's 2nd grade class was having a Mother's Day spring celebration, Juliet invited me only in a way that she could," Laurie, you're Alec and Ashie's mom but they're not here, but you are a mom to me when I'm not with my Mom so I think you should come so I can celebrate you too". How could anyone disappoint? Well, when I showed up, his ex-wife and her mother were as mad as two wet hens. I actually felt quite embarrassed for the scene that they made, thankfully while the children were outside rehearsing. I was sitting in one of those little elementary school chairs at Juliet's table when she lunged at me, shaking her finger in my face, " You know, you have some nerve showing up here", screamed the grandmother, "You're not Juliet's mother, this is for me, not you", chimed the ex. I just looked at the both of them in disbelief, as did the other parents. *Calm Laurie, calm, just stay grounded.* My response," The only thing that is important right now is that little girl who invited us all here to celebrate us, so we can address this later and away from Juliet but not here, not now". I was not going to be brought in to this craziness. I was not going to engage. I escaped without being assaulted but it was a close call.

It all started to unravel when Juliet came to me one night hysterically crying, and Juliet is one tough cookie. "I can't take it anymore, I'm sorry, I can't". Alejandro and Adele ran to us when they heard her cries, "What is Juliet talking about? What's the matter?". Juliet turned to Adele, "I'm sorry Adele, I can't lie anymore, I can't do this anymore". "It's OK Juliet, it's OK, you don't have to", Adele said as she wrapped her arms around her little sister. We all sat in Adele's room and they let it out, tears of sadness and guilt, the secrets. What they had confessed was shocking, it turns out that each time they return to their mother's house, they were interrogated about their stay, us, what we did, what we said, if they were hurt, had their arms and legs examined and concluded the third degree with their opinions of how horrible we are as people. They noticed their mother and grandmother's disappointment and disapproval when they had fun or enjoyed their time at our house, and sadly, as a result, they admitted that they had been making up lies and telling their mother horrible things about us and how we mistreat them because they thought it would make their mother happy. I felt so sad, for them, for us, for their mother. I felt empty, as if the little life that was left in me was once again being sucked out. Alejandro just sat silent as he wiped the tears from his eyes. After a long pause, he was only able to tell them that we love them and that it hurts him to hear them say that he would ever harm them. We weren't angry with the girls, they are children, innocent, just wanting to be loved and to love, to see their mom happy and stay out of the fray. In their little brains, if Mom is happy, then that's good, they are like little puppies looking to be pet; they didn't know about lawyers, judges, custody rights, or the ultimate, that they would be taken away from us. Boom, there it is. We comforted them and let them know that they cannot control their mom's happiness, only she can, and trying to only makes themselves unhappy. We are so proud of them as people, they are lovers and tried to love in the best way that they knew how. I can't imagine how resilient these little girls are, at 8 and 6 to go into an emotional war zone every other day.

We left it at that, we had to keep moving together and repairing our relationship and the core trust in our family. It was an injury but we made a pact with each other that night, 4 hands in the middle of our circle, that no one has the power to break us up or to make us not love each other. No one. It wasn't an option to spill the beans and inform the ex that this was all fabricated, no way, we would not throw the girls on the chopping block, and for what, so his ex could accuse us of bullying the girls into rescinding their accusations. We will take the hit. The girls, however, did not continue on with this path, all of the myths and fabrications about us stopped, no more complaints, even as infuriating as it was for their mother, the girls stayed true to themselves. In one report to the court, his ex-wife stated "not understanding, how could all of the sudden everything stop and the girls enjoy being with them?". Well we know why.

September 23, 2013, she threw down the gauntlet and filed for *Emergency Motion for Temporary Orders* to remove the children immediately from Alejandro's custody. She claimed that he was hitting them on the toilet so they couldn't escape until they were bruised and that I was making them pray to my dead children. The allegations are once again unbelievable, more unfounded, unsubstantiated accusations lacking any evidence or reports from any sources other than herself. Might I point out that still, in the midst of all of this, we were all still healing and adapting to the deaths of Alec and Asher. Juliet's healing was through her Ashie doll, it did not bring her pain to know that he was in heaven, and was the closest thing to him, an object of comfort, like a stuffed animal or fuzzy blankie. So when Juliet first went away to sleep away camp that summer for a week, she had asked if she could bring a photo of Asher to remind her of us and her family if she gets lonely or scared. "Of course you can love, we are all right here, even if you can't see us!". When Juliet returned from camp and we asked if the photo helped, she put her eyes down and said that she didn't take it. "What happened?". "My Mom ripped it up, she said that it was inappropriate for you to give me a picture of a dead baby." It's not enough that she is adapting to the death of someone who she calls now her brother, but to then try and take away her Dad? Even when I re-read these allegations four years later, I see what a pathological place they come from.

The Court's ruling: *Motion denied.* Another bullet dodged thanks to our attorney Mr. Seisco. The aftermath was filled with mandates from the court, one of them was being assigned a Parent Coordinator. We had the luck of being assigned, Mr. Sheenan, a former family court judge who was appointed to mediate high-conflict divorce relationships and act as an extension of the Court so the presiding Judge does not have to be burdened with nonsense or minor parental disputes. Now I have heard nightmare stories from my colleagues about the incestual web comprised of psychiatrists, therapists and forensic psychologists, parenting classes and "so called" experts who take advantage of high conflict divorces and weave a web of self referrals that is very hard to escape. Let's see, two wealthy Harvard grad physicians? Custody issues? High conflict? Gold mine. Our experience was no different. Regardless of the complaint, we perceived there to be a continual pattern of favoritism towards his ex-wife, painting her as the victim and blame seemed to be caste on Alejandro. It turns out that two months later, we discovered that Mr. Sheenan, nor his ex-wife's attorney disclosed to us or the Court that he was engaged or married to an attorney in his ex-wife's attorney's law firm. Can you say conflict of interest? Who's to say, but one cannot deny the possibility of his ex's attorney having a potential advantage or access to privileged and confidential information. Throughout all of the disputes and rulings, his ex and her attorney knew they had a potential advantage. We were all stunned by what was revealed, however, I assume that no one wanted to set this right more than the presiding Judge based on how quickly Mr. Sheenan was removed from our case. Emergency hearing: Ruling: *Immediate dismissal.* Thank you, there is such thing as justice.

It has been almost ten years since Alejandro's divorce, and let's just say that a tiger doesn't change his stripes and a scorpion has a stinger. Have the accusations lessened in severity, yes, but have they stopped, no. Not a chance, but we have accepted that this is an aspect of our relationship with his ex-wife and the divorce and have an excellent Parent Coordinator who has put structured parenting agreements around communications and parenting time. No one can control another person from waging war against them, but what we can do is our best to keep the girls out of the fray and in truth. This is reality, sometimes people get an amiable divorce, sometimes they don't. We didn't, but there is an understanding amongst the girls and us; their mother's feelings about us are none of our business, meaning we cannot control them, and nothing that we can or will do can or will bring happiness to her, only she can. Adele and Juliet are young women now, Juliet almost 12 and Adele 14, they are no longer babies or young children blindly swallowing anything that is presented to them. Yes, I am sure that they have battle scars, but how they use this experience to grow as a person, to channel their strengths and set boundaries for themselves and others is yet to be seen. Of course, it is painful for them to see their mother unhappy, and I love that they have this ability to be kind and show compassion, but the invaluable lesson learned is knowing that the gifts they have to offer anyone who is suffering is not pity or superficial attempts to force happiness but patience, loving-kindness and compassion.

So those are our ex's, both guilty of a crime, one for murder, the other for theft. One has murdered any spec of love inside of him, any chance of hope, dreaming, fun or human touch, the other has robbed herself of serenity, compassion, happiness and most of all, wasted those precious grains of sand that we are all allotted to her on resentment and vengeance. The punishment: imprisonment, one physically, the other psychologically.

I really don't know how I made it through sometimes, the threat of losing my family again, of being separated from the children. Amidst the psychological and legal battle, I was still a woman consumed with an incredible amount of grief and pain, trying desperately to adapt to the death of Alec and Asher. There were moments, especially after the girls shared their tales of woe, that I just wanted to throw my hands up and walk off the stage. I spent hours examining beliefs about his ex-wife, the children, divorce, family, the court system, unrelenting so I could find the truth of my thoughts and take the power away from their torturous grip. But that's the grit that lives deep inside all of us, you'll never know how much there is or how much you can tolerate until it is called upon. I had to fight with Alejandro to keep his children, for me to keep my new family, these girls who chose me as their parent, friend and confidant, these girls who loved me and I them. So there's the C- word again. No, not that one, Cancer. I had to see it the same as when I was diagnosed with Hodgkin's, except this time, I was dealing with the malignancy born from the untruthful thoughts of another person, resulting in an attack on our family and I was going to give it everything I got.

It was very painful and scary to think that we would lose custody, the presence of our children (again) or to not have an opportunity to have a relationship with them, but this experience actually had the opposite effect. Byron Katie taught me a very important lesson: if I, another person or the larger society/world can benefit from something, it can't possibly be bad. Painful yes, but not bad. And pain and bad are not synonymous. So was this painful? Yes. So here's the question: How did I, Adele, Juliet, Alejandro, our family, his ex-wife, the attorneys, Mr. Sheenan, the Judge, our friends benefit from it? Well, I believe that if one looks close enough and goes inside themselves, they can see that sometimes our adversaries hold some of the most valuable lessons.

This situation taught me just how important it is to examine my thinking. As Katie says," Thoughts aren't dangerous unless you believe them". Now no one likes to be attacked or threatened, but how could arguing with the nature of others possibly help me? If I did not meet my thoughts with understanding and find the truth of them, I could easily be consumed with anger, spite, jealousy and rage, transported to the same place as the ex's and I chose that I did not want that for myself. That is what I can control, to not live scared, to not use the children or others maliciously to serve my own agendas or interests, to see that those who are vindictive and insecure are suffering spiritually, internally, by their own perceptions of the world; it taught me that I am stronger than I knew.

But most of all, it taught me about the power of love. Sometimes the experience of the threat of separation actually brings people closer, and that is what happened with us. An attempt to separate us has actually galvanized our relationship. We had to walk through hell to get it, but ended up in the Garden of Eden. It's really quite ridiculous, if one was a fly on the wall and saw our family watching TV or sitting on lounge chairs at Big Surf, we are all snuggled up, practically sitting on top of each other.

Today, only because we have clarity on what we want for our lives, our wellness, and our happiness, and harboring resentments is incongruent. We refuse to be prisoners of our own mind as a result of what we believe should or shouldn't have happened or how one is or isn't supposed to be. Radical acceptance of what is, that is what facilitates our freedom. I am willing to withstand taunts, bullying and cruelty, hate and anger; I will stay strong and believe in myself, in living the life I want, for myself, my children and my family. So taunt me, bully me, for I will not move from what I believe in.

We have no hatred towards his ex-wife nor wish her any harm, we only have compassion and understanding in the suffering.

So I thank the girls' mother, without her, I would not have my daughters Adele and Juliet and an opportunity to be a mom again. Thank you.

TRIAL BY JURY

*In times of need, one should rise to the occasion
and fight bravely for what is right.*

- Dalai Lama

SEPTEMBER 17, 2012, the first day of the murder trial for Alec
and Asher, almost

2 ½ years after the death of the boys. It is so surreal even writing that sentence. Alec, Asher, murder, trial: I never imagined these words being sewn together. I've been asked a million times by everyone including myself, will you go? Should I go? What if I don't go? I have worked very hard to distance myself from the convicted, that is what I now call Andre.

Before the trial , I went to meet with Bill Montgomery, the County Attorney for Maricopa County, to discuss the State's position on a plea. Now it wasn't going to be a great one, but it looked like this: life in prison without the chance of parole vs. death. It wasn't the State that wanted to plea, it was me. Of course I wanted him convicted and to never be set free and truthfully, I really didn't and still to this day, do not care what they do with him. In my eyes, he is a piece of garbage. My reason for meeting with Mr. Montgomery was to discuss how we could avoid a trial,

I just didn't want my parents or myself to relive the crime, I didn't want to have to go back there. Mr. Montgomery was very kind, he generously met with Randy, my parents and I to answer any questions that we have and to listen to our position regarding the trial. However, as a West Point graduate and decorated Gulf War veteran, he makes it very clear, "Andre chose the wrong state to murder in, especially children and we will seek his life for that". I since learned that Arizona, as evidenced by Mr. Montgomery's vigorous position on upholding some of the toughest sentencing laws, is the harshest state regarding murder and the death penalty, only second to Texas.

My business, what I can control within myself, is to protect myself from information that I do not want to hear and that which I do, if I want to attend the trial and for how long, to work with the State prosecutors to make sure that this person is not free, ever. My goal is two prong: to have the opportunity to confront Andre and for him to hear that he is 100% responsible for the death of Alec and Asher and to obtain a penalty conviction detaining him for the rest of his life. I only want a conviction because he is dangerous, simply put: when he gets angry, he kills people. For me, this is not about revenge or justice, as there is no justice, nothing is going to neutralize or bring back Alec and Asher. I only want Andre to be imprisoned because it is the closest thing we have to take away his privilege of freedom and to protect us as a society.

I am feeling so uncomfortable as I enter the courtroom, it is so big, so serious, this is no longer Scottsdale municipal court where he has been before, defending a DUI or a reckless driving charge. My eyes immediately turn towards the defense table, his attorneys are present but he is not. I am dreading seeing him. Will he turn around and look at me? As I survey the room, like a modern day coliseum preparing to release the lions, I see television cameras in the back, ready to headline this heinous crime on the five o'clock news. On the defendant side of the court room sits Jeannette, Andre's mother and step father Rick, his uncle and a few strangers. I don't care to make eye contact with them, these were people who I once loved, that Alec and Asher called grandma and grandpa, now they are strangers. I don't know who they are or who they have become. Shells of people. I am humbled by the overwhelming presence of my family and friends, my best friend Pattie was passing out orange rubber bracelets with the words "Alec and Asher: Sewn Together". A band of brothers and sisters, gathering around me like white blood cells to a wound, united in love and a hope of recovery.

Ever since the boys died, I have been very protective of all information that is shared with me, because once heard, it is very difficult if impossible to neutralize or forget. I don't care to hear the details of the crime, for what? Do I really want or need to know how he killed Alec and Asher? And where? The evidence of his pathology? No. I don't want it or need it. I told others around me, especially my parents who moved here for three months during the trial, do not tell me details, if I want to know, I will ask the question. My litmus test in deciding whether to know something or not was this: Is it going to help me heal? If the answer was *no*, then my response was *no thank you, I don't want to hear this*. I have found that sometimes as humans, we are addicted to wanting to know, seeking to finding out as many details as we can, in other words, engaged in the gossip of the event.

Trial: Day 1: Bill Schutz and Kirsten Valenzuela were the lead attorneys, some of Maricopa County's best, a conviction rate that matched no other. From what I was told, Bill himself went out to the crime scene the day that Alec and Asher were killed, he wept and then turned to the Chief of Police and said, "I am taking this one, I have to".

Kirsten was a spicy Latina, with three boys of her own, you could see that she had to. She has moxie and was not one to be messed with. She made it clear after meeting with her in one of our countless pre-trial conferences, "Laurie, I can't bring the boys back but I want to make sure that every day Andre suffers, until the day that he is put to death. I want him to not even have the privilege of buying a week old burrito from the vending machine. I want him to understand that he lost the privilege of human touch (apparently when one is on death row, you cannot have visitors for a year and when you do, the glass that separates the convicted from the visitor is 5 inches thick). I want him to remember every day what he did. That is what I can do for Alec, Asher, your Mom and Dad and you".

I strategically sat on the end of the row, off of the main aisle, so I could get up and leave in an instant if I wanted or needed to. As I sit quietly, holding my Dad's hand, I see a door open off to my left side, it's him, walking like a penguin. He was dressed in a white dress shirt, tie and dress pants, as if he was going to hold an open house. He wasn't shackled which alarmed me, but he wasn't going anywhere. He had a hidden taser strapped to the inside of his thigh, one wrong move and he's going down. I can't take my eyes off of him, I just stare, thinking so many thoughts, *What happened to you? Look at you. I can't imagine what you are thinking or feeling? Was it worth it? Alec and Asher loved you.* I look away, only to see in front of the courtroom, the evidence sprawled out on tables of the crime scene; the couch cushions, the letters safely sealed in plastic bags, the gun. I can't do this. How am I going to do this. My thought is quickly interrupted by a door opening to my right, there they are, the jury, all 21 of them. It took four months to create this panel," *please protect us, please protect me,"* I thought to myself as I surveyed every single one of their faces. One juror in particular catches my eye and brings a slight smile to my face in amusement, a woman with the most beautiful orange hair, just like Alec. A Gingy. I think to myself, *Hi Alec, so you are here...* "All rise, the Honorable Karen O Connor presiding". It's starting, here we go. I stand, my eyes still fixed on him, as if my anger and disgust could bore a hole through his skin if possible. Twenty-two minutes. That's all I lasted. The minute I heard Kirsten starting to talk about how the paramedics attempted to perform CPR on Alec in her opening argument, I was out of there. It's too much. It is an image that I never want in my head.

My parents went every day, my Dad took three months off from his medical practice and all golf game invitations were declined by my Mom. As for me, I attended only a total of four days; the two days that I had to testify, the day I was permitted to make a victim statement and the final day of sentencing. My Mom had told me that she had promised herself and the boys that she would go every day, she would represent them posthumously. They would come home every night, careful not to report too much on their day, but it was tough, all of us were walking on eggshells. I don't know how they did it, to hear all of the details. Gratefully, we have an amazing support system, my Dad's best friend David, who our families grew up together with, came out from Miami and sat, side by side with my Dad for three weeks. Friends brought dinners, set up massages and texted me an orange, heart emoji every day.

There was one day that I offered to go, and that was the day that Angela had to testify, *Miss Angela* as Alec referred to her as. Angela joined our family in 2005, I was looking for a Mommy's helper and decided to put an advertisement in the State Press, Arizona State University's newspaper.

Wanted: Adorable, smart orange-haired boy is looking for a fun-loving, responsible and intelligent person to pick up from preschool, read books with and take to the train park". Monday-Friday, 3:00 pm-6:00 pm. Clean driving record, CPR/First aid certified, P.S.: Also needs to love cats!

Miss Angela with three other candidates answered our ad, but Miss Angela was it, she was perfect; only eighteen but had a great deal of maturity and emotional intelligence. Alec quickly took to her and considered this beautiful brown haired, blue eyed girl, his. I'll never forget the time when Miss Angela was babysitting, she had asked if her boyfriend Brian (now her husband), could come over and join Alec and her for dinner. When Brian walked through the door and kneeled down to shake Alec's hand, you could see the look, another suitor was on deck. Alec quickly rushed to show Brian his trains and engineered train track masterpieces.

Angela recollects that dinner vividly, Angela made her famous fajitas and to impress Brian and her, Alec ate them, onions, peppers and all! Now that was impressive, a 3 year old eating grilled vegetables. Over the years, our bond with Miss Angela and hers to us was familial. It was an interesting dynamic that organically unfolded, she took care of my baby while I was working and I, unexpectedly began to mother her. Let's just say that Angela came from a family where she needed to become independent early on, so when it came to seeking a parental perspective, be it with boys, graduate school, or just life, I was it, I was hers.

Our family: Angela, Brian, Adele, Me, Alejandro and Juliet

On the days leading up to the trial, my Angela, understandably, was besides herself, Alec and Asher were *her* boys and she felt the bottomless loss. As a mom, I just wanted to take away her pain, I wanted to rescue her, to save her from what she had to go through, but I couldn't. She needed to testify, she also needed to sit in front of Andre and tell the jury about this man who she once considered her family and her account of the days before the murders. With Brian and me by her side, my girl was brilliantly strong.

The day of my testimony reminded me of a similar day, long ago, that girl who stood in front of the mirror with pigtails, wearing a shirt that that says, "I make boys cry", kick boxing and screaming, "Bring it on". That is me, the same girl, just a different costume. Wearing a Thomas Pink black and white pin-striped shirt, black skirt, and patent-leather heals, I am called to the stand. I feel all eyes on me as I approached the witness stand with Alec's Thomas the Train shirt in hand, just like he carried Cow Cow to comfort him, so do I. Silence, one could hear a pin drop. I look directly at him and implant my eyes. *I am here you piece of shit, I am right here. You did not kill me. You don't have that power.* I spend the next six hours being peppered with questions from both the Prosecution and Defense, directing all of my answers to the jurors. I wanted them to see me, to hear me. I am talking to you jurors, not Andre, not the attorneys, to you. The next time I look at Andre will be when I am making my victim statement to the court. On the second day of the

trial, there was scuffling about in the court room. "Andre apparently became suicidal after your testimony yesterday so they had him on suicide precautions", Randy advised me. *What a baby. Painful, isn't it to see me, to hear me. I am Alec and Asher, I am a reminder of what you had and what you attempted to kill.* I thought to myself. After an hour delay, they brought Andre in, doing his penguin shuffle, apparently pissed because when you are on suicide precautions, you sleep on the floor in a cell, naked, no sheets, no pillow. Day two was more of the same, painful testimonial reflections of those days leading up to his crime.

One aspect of Andre which was not admissible in the trial as a defense was his mental capacity. When people hear of what Andre did, their first response is, "Oh my God, was he crazy, you have to be mentally ill in order to do something like this!?". Well, he's not. It's just that simple. Under the law, one cannot premeditate a crime and then claim a "momentary lapse of reason", one cannot know right from wrong and then say "I didn't know what would happen". Andre planned this for three days, wrote suicide letters with the boys signature, put up a sign on the outside of the front door and called 911 after he shot them. All of his actions, before and after the crime points to his mental capacity: not mentally ill. Sane. He even had a Rule 11 hearing to prove capacity, which according to Arizona law, the legislative intent of Rule 11 is to ensure that a defendant in a criminal action in this state shall not be tried and punished if he is unable to understand the proceedings against him or to assist in his defense. After murdering the boys and his botched suicide attempt, he called 911 to get emergency assistance. His self-inflicted bullet went through the underside of his mouth, blowing off part of his tongue and teeth and exited through his cheek. Pity, he used to have such a nice smile. I am grateful for this incompetency to complete his self-destructive act, for he is sitting trial, 100% in tact of all of his mental faculties and understands this reality. I often wonder how I would feel if he was successful in his suicide attempt. Would it be easier because I would not have to go through a trial? Live hoping that he would never be set free? Or would it be harder because I would not have the chance to confront him? That he would have gotten off, no penalty served, at least not here?

The trial has three phases: the trial (deliberation), the verdict, and the penalty (sentencing). It took two and a half years to get to these dates: December 18, 2012, the day he was convicted. December 19, 2012, the day he was sentenced to death. His plea from day one: *Not guilty.* When I first heard that, I went crazy. Not guilty?! What the hell is that? Is he really asserting that he is innocent? Randy had to break it down for me, Law 101: First of all, in capital murder trials, the State automatically enters in a plea of Not Guilty, as to prevent a dynamic of "suicide by State", kind of like "suicide by cop". It would be the easy way out and default to have the State kill you. Secondly, is the aspect of the burden of proof and victim's rights. Randy explained to me that it is because they want to ensure neutrality of the process, it is the burden of the State to prove beyond a reasonable doubt, that the defendant committed the crime. A verdict has to stand on its own merits, not out of pity or emotion. It seems lop-sided though, for example, the convicted has the right to speak to the jury directly but the victim (me which I do not ever call myself or identify with that term) does not. It's unfair, but then again, this place doesn't operate on fairness. Andre is limited in what he can say to the jury, he has the right to tell them what he wants them to know, however, the law does not allow him to ask for a specific punishment. He didn't care, when his time came, he was quivering like a baby, begging them to not kill him. Which I don't understand why not? Why wouldn't you want to be sentenced to death, to end your physical imprisonment and torture as quickly as possible? There is the part of me that screams inside, asking, *So you chose to kill Alec and Asher, you didn't give them a choice to live and now you have the balls to beg for mercy? Where was your mercy when you were standing over Alec and Asher with a gun to their head? You stupid idiot.*

There it is, the State rests, the defense rests. Now it is in the hands of the jury. Eleven minutes, that's all it took. It was unanimous, all 21 jurors: the verdict: *Guilty.* It was one of the fastest convictions in the history of the State of Arizona. I guess that is how obvious his culpability is and how well the State presented their case. Kirsten and Bob were not going to leave any stone unturned, every detail tended to, they had to, for Alec and Asher.

Now to the penalty phase, the question on the table is life in prison without the chance of parole or death. I have been asked numerous times by family, friends, strangers, "What is your position on the penalty once he is convicted? What do you want them to do with Andre?". My response has always been the same, "The minute he killed Alec and Asher, he became the property and business of the State of Arizona, not mine". What perplexes me is how a State that is anti-abortion be pro-death penalty. Oh well, that is for another time, another book. I do not care if Andre lives or dies, not because I have a moral or religious position on this matter, it is because I have worked very hard to disconnect myself from him as a person. As long as I am invested in his life, whatever that looks like, I am connected, and he is the last person that I want to live with.

Now that the jury has determined guilt beyond a reasonable doubt, they must deliberate the mitigating factors of the crime and then decide the penalty and present it to the judge. The jury, anticipating the aftershocks of guilt, delivered a verdict possibly as consequential to me as the death sentence. Verdict: Death. They are going to kill him, it will take an average of about fourteen years until they hook him up to the lethal concoction of poison. Outbursts of fear, pain, relief were heard throughout the courtroom, sounds of weeping, then silence. It is unconscionable to me what must be going on through his mind, what his mother must be thinking, at least I didn't know that my children were going to be killed. She does and she has to live every day leading up until the day that they kill her child. He will spend the remainder of his days in a cell: 11 feet, 7 inches by 7 feet, 9 inches, twenty-three hours a day, only to see sunlight for an hour. A walk around the yard might sound like a reprieve, but his cell is the safest place for him. From what I've been told, even the murderers and rapists believe killing children is a sin and they will see that justice and punishment is served *their* way. All eyes turn to the judge as she formally sentences Andre to death, then asks him if he understands his sentence. He acknowledges. The judge then thanks the jury for their service and excuses them. But it's not over, not yet. I get my day in court, literally.

It is painful as I go into the folder located in the back of my filing cabinet to retrieve this for my book, as it is what it is, a statement to the jury regarding the murder of Alec and Asher. Such a painful place to visit. I remember that day, the day I got my proverbial "day in court" to make a final statement, not a victim statement but an impact statement.

MS. VALENZUELA: Ms. Morales would address the Court.

THE COURT: All right.

MS. MORALES: Your Honor, I don't know if you know, but I never wanted a trial. And it's not because I cared about what happened to Andre.

On March 31st, 2010, when he murdered my kids, he no longer was my business. He was yours. And he was the State of Arizona's business. But I didn't want a trial because I wanted to protect my family, my mom and dad. But I didn't get that opportunity, and that's okay.

But I wanted to thank you for making this a just place so that my kids, their rights as citizens and as humans were protected. So thank you.

THE COURT: Thank you.

And then I turned to him. I walked straight towards him and looked him straight in the eye, the Bailiff flinched a bit, not knowing where this was heading or how far it could go. I was not afraid, yes, I was facing a murderer, but I am the Mother, fearless and convicted in what I was about to proclaim.

MS. MORALES: So to you... This is not a dialogue. This is not a conversation. This is a statement that I have waited almost three years to look at you and to tell you three things. I have never imagined that I -- 15 years after marrying you that I would be standing here facing you as the murderer of our children. And the fortunate part is that you didn't have the courage to finish your act of killing yourself, and that you have a brain that works, and you have eyes, and you have ears, and you have a conscience, Andre. You have a conscience.

You're not mentally ill. You killed our children. You are the stupidest person I have ever met. You're probably the stupidest person, and you know why? I will tell you why.

You're the stupidest person because I loved you. That's why you're stupid. Because I believed in you. We had nothing, and we championed each other. That's why you're the stupidest person. Because you killed -- Andre, you killed the two people who loved you. Alec loved you. He loved you, and you killed him. You killed him.

I'm not going to get into the lies and the deceit. That's what these people do. But there came a time when I chose not to have you as my partner. But I was always Switzerland, Andre, neutral. I never, ever, ever had any intention of hurting Alec or Asher like your mom hurt you. You never had that opportunity, and I promised you I would never do that. But see, you wanted me. You did whatever you wanted in our relationship and then had the arrogance to turn around and say, "Well, get over it." And then when you couldn't have me, you did what you were taught, and that was to hurt me. And you know that the only thing that I gave a damn about was Alec and Asher. I didn't care about anything else, but you chose to hurt me. And the stupidest thing is that why didn't you just kill me? Why didn't you just kill me? But you didn't. You killed Alec and Ashie, the babies.

You know, my happiness belongs to me. And I'm angry at you. I don't -- I do have hate for you. I do have hate for you. But, you know, I also have the ability to love. And I know that love will always, always conquer.

But my happiness does not lie within Alec and Asher. I can't or I'll die. It lies within me. And you couldn't take away my happiness.

If stupid was a crime, you would be 100 percent guilty. And you know what, Andre? My truth, my truth is that I am in no way responsible for the death of my kids. If I knew, at all, that those babies were in danger, I would do anything. I would have taken a bullet. That's how much I love my kids. But you didn't give me that opportunity.

You are 100 percent responsible for the death of Alec and Asher. And you know it here. You know it. I miss them every day, every moment, and I *know* that you miss them too. But my life has to be created again and I'm not going to die because of what you tried to do to me. And I'm not going to die because Alec and Ashie died. I will recover from this. But let me tell you who probably will not, and that is your mom. Once again, you hurt the only person who loved you, that stood in your corner. I don't have any sympathy for her, and you know why? I think that your mom is also one of the stupidest people, because she taught you that getting revenge and that being hateful and spiteful -- and you would tell me this -- is the way to be.

I don't wish anything bad on you. I don't. I wish, as my mom said, that you would have made different choices. You know, somehow in my brain I thought, God, if Andre is sorry, then maybe Alec and Asher will come back. But that's not how it works. They're never coming back. And neither are you. Neither are you.

You had us, but it's not the way that you wanted to have us. So now you are the property of the State of Arizona. And whatever your future holds, I don't wish you anything. I don't have any investment in whether you live or die, feel guilty or not, are harmed or safe, but I think that you are in for a horror of a journey -- it's unconscionable. And the most torturous part about your life is knowing that you murdered your kids. Animals don't murder their kids, recalcitrant murders don't even murder their own kids, but you did. And you did because you wanted to hurt me.

So, to that, I say you failed. I'm going on with my life. I will live well because I say so, because no one has the power to claim my happiness. There is not a God damn thing that I want to hear from you. There is nothing that you can say that I want to hear, need to hear, and am willing to hear that will make it okay, that will make me understand how you hurt and killed a 5-year-old and a 15-month-old baby that you were supposed to protect. There is nothing that you have to offer.

So I wish you good riddance. Wherever you go, you're on your own. You will never feel love again. You will never be hugged again. No one will ever care about you again. You will never have the privilege of choice, of freedom, that's your consequence. As for us, we are free.

Alec and Ashie didn't have a choice to live or to die, and you have the audacity to ask the jury for mercy. Where was the mercy, Andre? Where was the mercy when you held a gun to Alec? Where was it? You killed him. You gave him no mercy, and you gave Asher no mercy.

So you know what? Don't sit in front of a jury now, because you're facing the death penalty, and ask for mercy. You didn't give our children that opportunity.

You're asking for it because you don't want it yourself. Well, our children didn't have that choice. You have a lifetime of thinking, to ask yourself if it was worth it before you are the one being murdered, but for me, you died a long time ago.

THE COURT: Thank you, Ms. Morales.

MS. MORALES: Thank you, Your Honor.

I was done. I had said all that I wanted to say. I turned my back to him and walked out of the courtroom, one of the most powerful messages sent to him and to myself. I was incomplete, there was one last piece missing, the jury. Randy had given me a heads up that they wanted to meet with me privately after three months of holding their tongues. As I paced outside of the courtroom, the door to the jurors quarters opened. "They are ready Mrs. Morales", the Bailiff said. I humbly walked into the inner sanctum with a bag of orange Alec and Asher bracelets in hand. I humbly scanned the oval table of onlookers as I had done many times before over the past months. What are they about to tell me? What if I can't handle what they are about to tell me? After a long, pregnant pause and several guttural grunts in an attempt to contain his emotions, the foreman broke. "We've been waiting a long time to tell you this: You could not have known. We have seen all the evidence—even more than you have—and we firmly believe that you, that no one, could have seen this coming.". One by one, the jurors wept as they shared their thoughts and feelings as they put on their orange bracelets in solidarity for the boys, for me, for us, "We will never forget Alec and Asher, we will never forget you. For the rest of our lives, the color orange will never be the same, when we see orange, we will see Alec and Asher and smile and remember those beautiful boys of yours".

But the question persists, seethes. How could I not have known? As expected, years later, this belief is still alive, less powerful than before but still demands my attention. In retrospect, I see that he was driven by a voracious feeling of "never enough." He had a Mercedes E class, but he wanted an S class. He had modest success at trading so he took more risk—and lost our one hundred and eighty thousand-dollar savings. He had one eight-shot martini and wanted another. And another. Not just one prostitute—but, as he told me, twenty-seven. His keeping track was a horror in itself.

But he was never violent. And he was steadfast with the children. He was—although the thought is dizzying to even consider, knowing what I know now—a good father. He was a master of hiding evil in plain sight, perhaps hiding it even from himself. He bought the gun not in some secret dark-alley deal but at the Bass Pro Shop, the family-friendly outdoor adventure store where we took the boys regularly to feed the fish, marvel at the animal heads on the wall, and have chicken fingers for lunch. He walked through those same doors, abided the requisite three-day waiting period, and walked out again with the gun he would use to kill our boys.

I can reasonably demonstrate, and sometimes even believe, that I am not guilty. After all, the guilty party sits on death row, fully culpable. But the wily mother-brain scans and searches for punishment. Although the details of the crime have been fully documented and adjudicated, I still, at times, am left with a live-wire image of my boys looking up at me and asking, "What happened?". I know that answer, as I had found it many years ago within myself through the mechanism of inquiry. Truth was alive inside of me, a truth that is everlasting and independent of a judge, jury or judicial system.

That is my ending to the crime, but not his. The crime and sentence now belong to the convicted and the punishment to the State of Arizona. He no longer has a name, he is only identified as #277278 at Florence Prison. I will not show you a picture of him, as that image is yours to choose, if you so dare to have that in your mental photo library. However, I leave you with this statement: he still serves one purpose for us. Him and others sitting on death row remind us how not to live and to recognize how powerful our thoughts are. He reminds us to respect the power of the ego and thoughts born from it and the responsibility that we have to question everything, if not, it has the potential to incarcerate and kill, an insidious murderer of our dreams, our freedom, and ability to love.

I guess even a convicted murderer can offer teachings if we are paying attention.

PART FOUR

REFLECTIONS

Bottom of the Brainstem

*The true value of a human being can be found
in the degree to which he has attained liberation
from the self.*

-Albert Einstein

No one could have explained or prepared me for how my brain was or is after the death of the my children, being diagnosed with cancer, getting pregnant (again) or hearing the number, "27". And I am not just referring to deceit or death, trauma is idiosyncratic to us as individuals, it could be a sudden break up or divorce, finding out that your partner is gay or your child is not who you want them to be. Trauma was not about what happened, it is uncovering and understanding the beliefs about what has happened. All are traumatic, in their own ways, all ground-zero for our brain, all sharing a common similarity, they violate our idea of safety and security about the people and the world, leaving us in a place of unfamiliarity, insecurity and doubt. This is what can complicate grief and undermine our ability to adapt to a new life, a different life.

Am I losing my mind?

No, you are not. Now we are not going to get too clinical, but here is our brain on trauma: the amygdala is part of the brain, centered very deep within the brain , its primary role is in the processing of memory, decision-making, and emotional reactions and helps us identify what is safe and what is dangerous. Important job. So, where does it get it's information from? The memories of the past. What that means is that when we are faced with a situation, it looks backwards in order to assess the present or future situation with. Think about it: you eat at a restaurant that you have frequented many times before, it's always been delicious. But this time, you end up getting food poisoning, vomiting and diarrhea for days. Pretty traumatizing. Fast forward, a friend asks you to dine at the restaurant for dinner, in an instant, you reference the past memory and a decision is made ,"I'd love to dine with you but not there!". You may also have experienced the power of the amygdala, as it is wired into that frontal lobe (our "forehead part" that our cats and dogs don't have). Based on its findings, it creates thoughts about what is and what we think it means. In our example of the restaurant, it may conjure up other thoughts such as "It's dirty there, they probably don't buy quality ingredients or their food isn't prepared correctly". A traumatized brain sounds like this, " Don't do it, this happened before so it's going to happen again!". Hence, our future is crafted on this pattern, of course, unless we do something about it. Now maybe it's no big deal, we just won't go back to that restaurant, but imagine if an entire gender is seen as dangerous? Or relationships? Or this world? All of the sudden this place, it can feel pretty claustrophobic and overwhelming. We must be careful because our seemingly small stories can turn into bigger stories and all of the sudden, they become our ideology for our life and this world that we live in.

Now, while the brain is freaking out, being all-consumed in survival mode, it is disorganized, forgetful, easily startled, and confused, as it should be. That, of course on top of having flash-backs, avoiding people and places that remind you of the event and being hyper-aroused (jumpy, easily startled). Our attention is a limited resource, so if the brain is attending to perceived danger, it is not going to be paying attention to locating the dry cleaners that you have had for twenty years, keeping track of your car keys, or bothered with "what's for dinner". I recall the first months after Alec and Asher died, I was traveling north on Scottsdale Road when I thought that I was traveling south, nothing looked famil-iar, I couldn't understand why I could not find the grocery store that I frequented for the past thirty years. It felt so scary to be that disoriented, I felt as if I had lost my mind (Well, technically I did, temporarily).

We must remember to be gentle with it, it is trying to help us and is very confused, but there is an invisible "occupied" sign on your forehead. Kind of like the colorful kaleidoscope circle that appears on your computer screen when it freezes. It is pre-occupied with the belief that the world is completely dangerous and no one can be trusted, and for some, not even God. We are convinced that the earth will once again open up and engulf us, because that is what it feels like. The only difference is that it's not true: we were spared, left behind, or narrowly escaped. I de-scribe it like this: One day, you decide to go to the beach, just as you have done many times before. Your loved one and/or you are swimming in the ocean when all of the sudden, a shark attacks, you somehow make it back to shore. There you lie, injured, gasping for life, when you suddenly realize that your loved one did not make it. They are dead. You begin desperately screaming at the water for them to somehow miraculously appear, but there is nothing, just an eerie silence. This is how it feels the moment one is exited from their life as they knew it, before the entrance into hell.

Grounding:

It's alright and quite frankly, expected, to not want to go back into the ocean, or even visit the beach. But what is more scary, more painful than going back in the ocean is sitting on the shore, hijacked by your brain, not living the life that you want to live, especially if you love the swimming. So, we go, slowly towards the water. While we are inching towards this new life, we must be encouraging to our brain about what is going on right now and we do this through "grounding" exercises. Grounding is a simple exercise that roots a person in the here and now, in reality, and that will directly help lower our amygdala from freaking out. We can ground ourselves by describing physically what we are perceiving. For example, I feel the wind and my hair blowing on my face, the sand is mushy and soft on my feet, the water is cold. Cognitively, we can ground ourselves through the use of repetitive thoughts," One foot in front of the other, slow, slow, one foot in front of the other, slow, slow". Check in with yourself, " How are we? That wasn't so scary. I am still here, the ground is supporting me, I am not injured". Then keep moving, repeating the same steps, moving at your pace. Talk to yourself, giving this brain feedback. "I see water, I see waves, I see kids playing in the sand". But make sure that you don't shift to thoughts that are not true, meaning based in reality such as ," Everything will be OK" or "Nothing dangerous is going to happen". I caution you about these thoughts not because they are not kind or gentle, it's just that your lizard brain will not believe them and actually, might become more anxious. These beliefs are future-oriented and as we have learned, the future is uncontrollable and unpredictable, that is why they are untrue, hence, your mind will call bullshit on them. Stay present, in reality with thoughts such as," Look at us, we are OK right now", or "Nothing dangerous is happening right now", and that feels less stressful, less scary.

Support the Support

You never know how strong you are until being strong is the only choice.

- Dad

O NE OF THE FIRST TASKS that I had to do in supporting my-self was to teach these kind-loving people who were gathering around how to support me. Not that I was in a place to take on anything, but I needed to gain some semblance of direction over what, when, and how things were occurring for and towards me; how I wanted them to "show up", what I wanted them to do or not do, talk about or not talk about. Our supporters don't know, how could they, we may not even know ourselves! None of us have been through this, and if they have, it wasn't with us. Everyone as individuals, have their own ideas of what support and comfort looks and feels like, what is an irritant and what is comforting, and is a fluid, ever-changing state. We might even find ourselves only being able to identify what we don't want and not what we do want.

My words of wisdom to the loving- supporters (and you have to trust me on this one), it's OK to tell the injured person that you have no idea how support looks to them, but you are present and open to whatever that looks like for them. You don't have to have all of the answers or know what to do, it may be even more powerful and calming for all to humbly admit that you don't, but you're here to do whatever or you'll figure it out. It might change from minute to minute, day to day, or they may not even know, but you will hold the space until it comes to them.

We may all agree on that statement, but how do we do it and what does that look like? Here is how I found my "new brain" on April 1, 2010 and some techniques that I came up with that helped the amazing people who gathered around me:

To talk or not to talk, that is the question:

One skill, that once we thought as effortless and quite basic, is the ability to talk. As mentioned, sometimes the traumatized brain has a difficult time remembering or recalling words or thoughts. Sometimes it can be unbelievably scary just to say a word, for fear that the minute it comes out, all of one's thoughts and feelings will come dashing out, like an evil genie that we will be unable to be put back in the bottle. And how can I process something that I can't remember or even put into words? And what happens when there is a tragedy? These genuinely loving and compassionate people in our lives gather around to love on us, they want to talk about it, but that is the last thing that we are capable of doing, it may actually be more traumatizing and re-injuring.

For example, I wanted people to text, not call. Speaking was too hard for me, I couldn't gather my thoughts, some thoughts were too painful, it took too much energy and effort to talk; at times, the words just couldn't come out. Verbal conversations were way too unstructured and personal, whereas texting was more controlled and felt more private, no one heard me crying or was watching me, there wasn't an awkwardness because of a paucity in thought or conversation. I didn't have to worry about taking care of others' feelings, afraid that my grief or present form would scare them.

Emoji's:

Sometimes, (I said *sometimes*), emojis are the best invention ever. I could just text an emoji when someone asks me how I am doing, these were my top 3: , , . I could do *this*, I could communicate this way. But if someone were to call and ask me how I was doing, I would either be speechless or the words would grip me. Sometimes brutally aggressive thoughts would come to me, I would swell up with intense anger and want to scream, *How do you think I am doing, I am pretty messed up, my kids are dead, I don't have a home to call my own, I sat for hours today in the same place except to go to the bathroom, and I call myself only by my first name because my last name is that of a murderer. So how do you think I am doing?* Yeah, emojis were much better at that time.

I'm not proficient at mathematics but I'm great at numbers:

I taught them that I would love answering the question, *"How are you doing"* with a number. So, instead of answering with feelings, I answered with " I'm a 3 today". I began to describe what "3s" look like and how they are different than a "2". For example, a "3" may be able to wake up, not wanting to be here but will commit to living here another day, we brush teeth, shower, get dressed, eat breakfast, tidy up the house or go for a walk or on a short outing such as picking up a few things at the grocery store, whereas a "2" does not want to be here among the living today, maybe would not tend to their hygiene, would not be able to go outside the house, or sit in the same place or sleep most of the day.

It seems elementary but that is how we are recovering, sometimes starting with the basics. It allowed me to be in control, and that is a huge thing when you feel that you've lost all control of yourself. Any act of coming back into your own business, meaning what you can control in yourself, is a small victory. On a neuropath way level, it actual helps your brain "repave" the pathways that carry safe/danger messages and begins to weave them together, hence the "it's OK" pathways start to get stronger and take immediacy over the "let's get the hell out of here" pathways.

Holding the space:

"Thawing" is the process of becoming un-paralyzed from a traumatic experience. It is the time that it takes us to begin to come out of the shock of what happened and reconnect to this new life that we were dropped into. How long it took us to (*fill in the blank*); stop crying every day, all day, sit in one place for hours at a time, go back to work, make love to our partners, put on makeup, listen to music, go into their room, donate their clothes, visit them, make their favorite dish or visit their favorite place.

I have been asked by many supporters what they should do when the person who has been injured doesn't want to "move", physically and metaphorically. To them, I share these perspectives:

Timing is idiosyncratic to the person. There is no algorithm or prescribed steps that one "should" take, or stage that one is expected to enter in hopes of "moving along" or being able to process grief and predict our abilities. It is so valuable for our supporters to "hold the space", sit with us without trying to move us, be patient with us, and whatever happens, don't leave us! (even if it feels like we are pushing you away). For example, a friend might ask you to go for a walk or to sit outside at the local Starbucks and sip a coffee which might sounds nice to the grieving person, but it may take them 10 minutes to respond. Remember, right after you ask them, they are conducting a mini-root cause analysis of the offer: what will happen? Who will I see? Will I break down in public? What if I panic? Does this mean that I am expected to do more after this? It's all of this. As a supporter, this calls for patience, a grieving brain sometimes moves at the pace of a sloth, and everything, and I mean everything, is harder, slower and more painful than ever imagined. Wait, we will answer, just hold the space for us. And if we say no, don't stop offering, it might take us 10 times of being asked before we are able to engage.

Push and Pull:

Holding the space is an exercise in honoring where one is at, however, it is also important to acknowledge the importance of stretching ourselves and allowing our supporters to challenge us in facilitating our adaptation. We can maintain control by going at our pace, not moving at the pace that you think others want you to be. However, we also must temper this position with giving permission to our supporters to push us. We have to, they have to, they are our external motivator, our external propeller when we are unable to propel ourselves. Imagine if you had a stroke, you were unable to speak, express yourself or move. You were not paralyzed permanently but the deficits were far reaching in every aspect of your life. At first, you might feel hopeless and want to give up, recognizing that you are not going to die and living here like this is the worst option of the two. You muster a team around you of physical, occupational and speech therapists, your loved ones are right in there, cheerleading, cajoling, encouraging you every step of the way. Psychological recovery from a traumatic injury is no different. We have to push ourselves and we must let our team members push us as well. But remember, be gentle and sensitive, with yourself and others. How would it feel if you were being pushed too hard, by yourself or your supporters? How would your supporters possibly feel if you stopped trying? Frustrated? Scared? Powerless? We are all learning; what is important is to continue to openly communicate and trust that we all have a common goal: getting relief from the suffering and living a new life, a different life, whatever that could or may look like.

The Fish Bowl:

One of the most overwhelming aspects that I experienced when the boys died was knowing that there was thousands of conversations swirling around me, about me, for me. I could only imagine stories that were being told, I would probably have been thinking the same. Why did he do it? How could she not have known? What is going to happen to her now? I knew that I had made the headlines, in the news and in private conversations, like it or not, I was the goldfish in the bowl. We are spectators, whether we like it or not, this is an aspect of our makeup, we are a voyeuristic animal, as evidenced by our rubber-necking at accident scenes or love of reality shows. We certainly don't mind when the reviews are favorable or supportive and aren't so bothered when the gossip is complimentary or filled with adoration. But how do we respond when we find the comments to be irritating, when it is perceived as negative or scary, or impatient and insensitive?

I believe that I am loved by so many onlooking to see how I was going to survive this or searching for inlets of opportunity to support me. Simply living was a bonus. I would continuously hear these words, "You are so strong, courageous". I would graciously respond with a "thank you for your kind words" but privately, this was foreign to me. Courageous? Brave? How could one possibly be brave when this was not of my choosing? So I am brave to live? I think not. I see my strength in my decision to not suffer, to somehow figure out a way out of this straight-jacket, not just sit there, bound, trapped, waiting to be freed. That is strength. Now let's talk about courage. Courage comes from a belief that allows me to venture out, into an unfamiliar place. I lost my fear the minute that I realized the boys died. What was there to fear when the worst thing has already been experienced? So I guess you can call it courageous, but this is a really important piece to know: the reason why I chose to live a new life, a different life, is not because I am brave or strong, it's because I am stubborn. And stubborn is great sometimes. There was so much out of control around me, I felt as if I was being pushed around, a recipient of circumstances, that I had to grasp for the one thing that I could control, my choice to live.

When we come into this world, we don't get to choose to be here, to be born, to live. We don't get to choose our birthday. When we experience a trauma, everything is leveled, we are left like the mangled steel remains of the Twin Towers. So this is the question, the challenge that stands in front of all of us once we are leveled, however that comes; when did or will you make the decision to live? To choose to be here not because you were thrown into this thing called life, not as a result or because of someone else's choice but to be here as a volunteer. To choose to be here. Our first go around, we don't get that choice, but our second opportunity to live can be different. Some choose not to; to continue to drift along, like a piece of driftwood being carried, aimlessly and directionless by the currents of the ocean. Others choose to swim, to strategically put themselves in a direction, not because the destination is known, but because it is simply too painful to abdicate. For me, I chose to live, to be "born again" on September 24, 2010. That is my secondary birthday. That is my day that I chose to live. So maybe the choice to live a second time around *is* about courage and strength.

The Calendar

Live here, now, after all, we can't live anywhere else.

THIS THING CALLED the calendar is such an interesting invention. The simplest calendar system just counts time periods from a reference date, a timekeeper. But it's more than that, it is a storyteller. It is a man-made object that is made up of boxes with numbers in it, all containing a story about something or someone that has or is expected to occur. It is a symbol , just like everything: people, places, things that holds a meaning, a belief, a story. Before my trauma, I used it effortlessly just like a lot of other people, as a way to organize my work or social events, it was not painful, I actually enjoyed it. I used it to count the number of weeks that I was pregnant, the time until I get to drive, when I had a playdate or party, but it took on a completely different meaning and feeling after Alec and Asher died. I was trapped. It was a death tracker. I felt that this entire world was obsessed and subservient to the calendar, everywhere I looked, there was a reference to the keeping track. If I went into Target or the grocery store, the displays were of Valentine's Day, Halloween or Christmas, the television honored milestones from graduating diapers to getting married. After March 31st, all I saw was the number of days that I have been apart from them, or the time since I did (fill in the blank) with them. It also tracked the milestones that they did not experience, Asher's second birthday or Alec graduating from middle school. Or how about what they would have looked like now? Talk about torture, just pull out the knives. So let's take a closer look at this thing called the calendar.

Our house butts up against an Arabian horse ranch; these animals are magnificent, every morning they are let out to pasture to stretch their legs and frolic with each other. In the first weeks after the boys died, I would gain comfort in visiting the horses, that is when I mustered up enough energy and courage to take a walk. I would call them over to the fence and pet their long nose, admiring their huge eyes. I would look into these beautiful windows to their equine soul and ask them, "You don't know that it is April 6th, do you, that it is one week since my boys died? You don't even know that it is a Wednesday. Or that is it morning". It hit me, that so much of my pain was from thoughts surrounding dates, days, numbers, all referenced from the calendar. How would it feel if I no longer subscribed to the calendar? Can I do that? Why not, after all, there are no rules about how to *live* in this place, right? Children do and look at how happy they are? Playing, having fun, clueless to what is going on or how long it will last. Others do too, we just say that they are " off the grid" or disconnected from society. But I don't think so, maybe they are on to something? And is that necessarily a bad thing to do?

I imagined how I would feel, what my pain level would look like if I couldn't monitor the days since I was with Alec and Asher. It brought me such relief. So I did it, I went off the grid by renegotiating my relationship with the calendar. Now, it took some time, but I was clear, I no longer was willing to be a death tracker because every time I did, it was killing me, it would bring me swirling back into hell, the place where I was trying so tirelessly to walk out of. Here was my deal, I decided to only use the calendar to remind myself of the agreements that I had made with others or myself to show up. Dinner dates, programs that I want to watch, meetings at work. This felt manageable.

Birthdays:

birth·day 'bərTH͵dā/ noun

"the anniversary of the day on which a person was born, typically treated as an occasion for celebration and the giving of gifts, the day of a person's birth or the anniversary of something starting or being founded.

By definition and in practice, birthdays sound like so much fun and they were for me before March 31st, 2010, however, after a trauma, they are the antithesis, it is a "death day", the day that hell on earth was born. I have 2 birthdates, 2 days on the calendar that initially kidnapped me: December 8th and December 17th, Alec and Asher's birthdays. But what *is* it? When I started to look closer at these dates, these boxes with an "8" and a "1" and a "7" in it, what was the story? I came so close to the truth that I could feel God, this was a story of life and love, not death, pain or separation (well except for labor and delivery pains). These were the days that Alec and Asher were delivered to me, that life appeared, it was life looking at its own image. I love their "birth" day and all of their birthdays; turning one and mashing their face in the cake, opening up presents, running after balloons with their friends.

I loved it all. So why is this now a day covered with death? My answer, it's not. I had to preserve it in its original form. This is a day to celebrate my kids, so how am I going to do that in this new life? For me, the answer was clear, I am going to celebrate Alec by going to McDonald's and ordering his favorite: a happy meal. I could hear him ordering it as if it was yesterday, " I'd like bread, steak and cheese please and a boy's toy, not a girl's". (This was Alec's rendition of a cheeseburger). And to celebrate my Ashie? Hot dogs. I could see him now, just as I remember him on our last day together at the Arizona Science Center. How much closer could I possibly get to them? How else could I celebrate them and how happy I was on the days past which had the same symbols, "12/8", "12/17"?

What makes birthdays so painful for people who are grieving is the hidden story (sequence of thoughts) that is being transposed onto the date. They are treating this celebratory date as the death date. And it isn't! I have been in this place before, I am enjoying the moment and boom, in an instant, thought appears, " Alec would have been six, Asher should have been turning 2, it's not fair, I want them back, they should have lived until 90" and there we have it, the insane brain is off and running in hell. The only way to stop it in its tracks, to write down the thoughts and do The Work. Mine looked like this:

So, it's just not true, Alec was not supposed to be six and Asher was not supposed to be two, if they were supposed to, they would have. Remember, it doesn't mean that I like it, it just puts an end to any confusion that I have about their birthdays. And it brings awareness to another Master belief that all events being tracked have in common:

MASTER BELIEF: "It's not enough".

This belief says," I want more". And what happens to us when we believe this thought, with anything? I want more time, more money, more sex, more hair? It makes us feel desperate, anxious, preoccupied, controlling: let's just call it suffering. It instantly takes us from our present state of happiness and transports us into being preoccupied and obsessed with controlling future outcomes. We disappear. I don't know about anyone else, but when I am in this wild state, I don't show up as good as if I was calm, centered and having fun. Let's go deeper. So, is the belief that "more is better"? Along these lines of thinking, people who are older or live until 90 are happier and people who die at 15 are not? Is that true? You got it....NO! We can see when we vet the belief against reality, our theory is starting to quickly crumble. We might even find it laughable.

I remember when I was called in for a psychological consult at the hospital; Hilda was a 96-year-old woman in great health, she was fortunately only admitted for dehydration, but she was tearful and depressed. When I asked her what was paining her, she told me that today was her daughter's birthday," She should have lived as long as me, she didn't live long enough". Now, knowing the age of Hilda, I assumed that this was a sudden death from tuberculosis or childbirth. I asked her how old was her baby to which Hilda replied," my baby was 78". I just chuckled inside as I related to my own identical belief. After reflecting with Hilda, we both became a bit clearer with the truth in the turn-around: It is enough, it has to be because that is all we got, and when we desire more than what is given, we suffer.

Discovering and decoding this belief, "it's not enough", the question arose, "Enough for who?". For Hilda or her child. Is it possible that it would not have been a fruitful or happy life if Hilda's child had more time? Or if Alec or Asher had more time, maybe they would not have been happy with their lives or with me? So who are we to determine that more is better and more will make us happier? Who would I be without this thought, without the "back story", meaning a story behind the story? A girl sitting at McDonald's eating (sorry to say), a less than nutritious or savory meal, with a smile on my face. Literally and figuratively, eating a "Happy Meal".

That is enough for me...

MARCH 31sts

*"When a loved one dies, they are gone. So let them go.
Didn't you love them fully while they were here? Didn't
you share joy and laughter with them? When something
dies, let it. It is the nature of this world.*

- Barbara Ann Kipfer

EVERYONE WHO HAS LOVED someone that has died has one, it is inescapable: a death date. That's all it is. It is not a celebration of their life, it is not an "angel anniversary" as some like to call it, it is a day of death. Mine is March 31, 2010.

As I write on this day, it happens to be March 31, 2017, 8:04 a.m., my seventh one. How ironic. Not to get too religious, but all of the religions are littered with the symbolism of seven, being the foundation of God's word, the number of completeness and perfection (both physical and spiritual) and derives much of its meaning from being tied directly to God's creation of all things. In the Old Testament, there are seven days of creation, seven days of Passover, there are 7 days in a week and God's Sabbath is on the 7th day. In the New Testament, the Bible, as a whole, was originally divided into 7 major divisions; there are seven last sayings of Jesus on the cross. In Hinduism, there are seven chakras. I could go on and on; all of the Masters resonate seven. I guess for me on my seventh year, it is the year that I am able to share my completeness, my re-creation born from my destruction.

March 31st is the day that marks in our mortal way, how long it has been since I have been with Alec and Asher, at least here, in the physical world. Last night, I felt it, the dread of "its" arrival, not as much as last year or the year before, and definitely not anywhere near as painful as the first one. What was I dreading? I don't feel this dread for the waking of any other day of the year? Interesting question to ponder. I mean really, why is this day different than any other? Than March 3rd? July 29th? October 10th? Not to be crude but they weren't alive on those dates.

I know that my lizard brain is putting together one plus one and coming up with three. It is prepared to spend the entire day focused on memorializing what symbols it is seeing. It has even officially named it, like a Masters of Ceremony, "I hereby officially appoint March 31st as the "re-death" of Alec and Asher. We need to honor Alec and Asher, so let us only feel sad and somber, we must not feel joy or happiness on this day." Activities include crying, sitting in a trance, pushing our loved ones away and watching videos of their death, of course, like any good movie (or bad), there are sequels. It unconsciously does this and then calls it honoring. This even sounds bizarre just writing it!

But this is not true, it is impossible, there is only one "that day". Today is a day that has similarities to the day when Alec and Asher died, but they will not and did not die today. If that's the case, then I'm out because I never want to live that day again. Subsequent death days hold many similarities to that first death day. For example, today, the temperature when I wake, the sun is shining, I wake next to Alejandro, open my eyes and think of my boys, my body looks and feels the same as before, I know that it is springtime, Adele and Juliet are at their other house. If I were to look on a calendar, I would see a box with a 3 and a 1 in it, titled "March". However, this day has more differences than similarities if I sit still and look closer: it is a Friday, they died on a Wednesday, I do not wake to Andre calling my phone or my neighbor Wendi telling me that the SWAT team is at Andre's house. Instead of rushing to a crime scene, I am calm and relaxed, and walk downstairs, greeted by my cats and am sitting outside in my Buddha garden sipping coffee; Alejandro is making his famous eggs in the kitchen and I smell pomegranate scones baking in the oven. It is not that day. So which morning would I rather be in, the one in 2010 or 2017?

I remember my first (not that first), my first March 31st. It was 2011 and I had spent days anticipating its arrival. I had heard about this well-known beach called the " Anniversary" and the legacy of its deadly riptide, waiting to drown me. I was wading off its shoreline, just learning how to swim once again when suddenly, I feel it's pull, kicking up my legs, sucking me under, gasping for air. That of course didn't happen, but that was what I believed would occur. Alejandro was scared too, although he wouldn't admit it. He purposefully planned a trip for us so that we spent the first death anniversary far away, no familiar sights, no cell phones, no condolences. That was the closest thing he could give me, to transport me to another physical reality, in the hopes of easing my mind. Did it work? Yes, it definitely was helpful. It was temporarily taking me out of that ocean and putting me in a calmer sea. Now that didn't take away the pain but it lessened it, it took me to a place where I felt closer to Alec and Asher, in nature, with the wind blowing on my face as I breath them into my lungs, just as I did when I smelled their hair or supple baby skin. Where I lived, no different than others, was laden with symbols. Take my pick: the train park, my SUV that I bought for us as a family, certain streets, restaurants, places and faces, climate, it all held a story and just like a newborn born into a new life, I needed to be treated with kid gloves. In doing so, I needed to shield myself from these seemingly countless, powerful symbols or I would be short-circuited. Some people have asked, isn't that running away? My truth, yes. But what does that mean, running away? In order to run away, we must also be pursuing something. And is it necessarily a destructive choice? For me, it speaks to my emotional intelligence. I know that sometimes I need to distance myself from a story until I am able, willing or ready to look at it, to find the truth of it.

Seven years later, I no longer need to leave, hide, excuse myself or find a distraction to live here, or should I say, through March 31st. I no longer cringe at the thought of its arrival, bearing down all day, hoping and wishing that time would be kind and pass quickly. It is not just a matter of time passing by that has allowed me to live in such a peaceful place in my mind, because we all know a person who is stuck in that day. The mother who hasn't moved a thing from their child's room since the day that they died 11 years ago or the spouse who refuses to begin to date or is still wearing their wedding ring 21 years later. Stuck, back there. Standing right at the last minute that the physical separation occurred. If it was just a matter of time going by and pages flipping on a calendar, grief work would be a passive, effortless phenomena.

That day, just like all of the other days that came and went and those days that lie ahead of me, can only occur once. That day will never come again. Thank God. Isn't this place amazing how it is set up, the future comes, it is here for a brief moment and then it is gone, an infinite conveyor belt. I never want to relive March 31, 2010 again. Ever. Truth is the only way that I can relive that day is in my mind, if I pull up that video in my mind and replay it. The perception of the mind is the only place where one's reality lives. That day can't come again, it is the video of that day that scares me, the movie titled "The Murder of my Kids". Who wouldn't be terrified and seeking to run away?

So, here's the million dollar question: "How do you get the video of that day to stop playing?". Answer: by meeting the beliefs about that day with understanding. Understanding and finding the truth about the thoughts that comprise the story of events leading up to March 31, 2010. Once the mind has truth-based answer to its question, "What happened?", it will settle down, it will rest. That is not to say that I will ever like what has happened on that day, but my mind no longer has this involuntary reflex to go on a quest, summoning up videos for clues to find answers to the question posed. If or when it brings me that video, I just meet it with understanding, it is just trying to help me, like a dog bringing a treat, sometimes it's a bone, sometimes it's a poisonous snake. It is as if I am having a conversation with myself, I am my own guide and the one who needs guidance. Sane mind has to direct insane mind. For me, it looked something like this:

Image appears, it's of Andre's house, police, yellow tape, helicopters. I see Alec lying on the family room floor, I see Asher in his crib, both deceased. (Note: I NEVER saw them in the house, it is all my imagination of what I THINK I would have seen).

Thought appears after the image: " I'm sorry I couldn't save you. I love you so much my sweet babies. I want to be with you.

I want you here. Please come back. How could he do this? I just love you. I want to be with you."

Response: "I know Laurie, I know. I know this is so painful watching this. I know that you love them. They love you. So you want to be with them. Is that true?"

Response: "Yes, I do, I want to be with them. I want to see them smiling, playing trains, happy, alive."

Response: "Yes, Ok, so are they alive in this image?"

Response: "No, they are gone."

Response: "OK, good, so it is impossible to connect with them, isn't it? You are only connecting with the image of death, whether you saw it with your own eyes or not, and when we are not connected with them, they are "gone" aren't they?"

Response: "Yes."

Response: "Well if you want to connect with them, then let's go to them, let's go to where they are, in an image of them because they are not in this video, this is a crime scene, a murder movie. Not the video of Alec and Asher."

Response: "Do you want to be in a murder movie of Alec and Asher?"

Response: "No. No."

Response: "Then let's go. They are not *there*, they are *over here*."

It is a conscious redirection, and that is work. But there is no option, I am not going to sit and watch a murder movie for 24 hours. The mind, without resistance, will follow, like a little child being escorted away from the edge of a pool or a dangerous street. I no longer let my brain get away with whatever it wants, and it is not through strong-arming it, distracting it or shutting down, it is only through a gentle process of meeting it with patience, loving-kindness and empathy. The mind will begin to stop featuring these traumatic videos when it is met with understanding and no longer is attaching to a thought that is not based in reality. ("I'm sorry I couldn't save you"). Decoded, this belief says, "I should have known. I have the power to save you. Mothers are supposed to predict danger and because I didn't, I failed them". This is what we need to do inquiry on, all of these beliefs that comprise the story, a.k.a., the movie. Once the mind finds truth, like a homicide detective, it settles down, case solved.

SURVIVOR GUILT

"There is nothing clever or honorable about not being happy".

ONE OF THE BARRIERS to walking out of hell, or staying out is the feeling of guilt. As humans, we really don't have that many original thoughts, they have all been thought before us and if we have thought of them before, they are usually regurgitated and revisited streams of thinking. Feelings of guilt are born from thoughts that may sound something like this:

"It's dishonoring them if I am enjoying myself or feel/get some relief."

" If I am happy, it means that I've moved on or that they don't matter anymore"

"They didn't get more time so why should I?

"If I am happy, it means that I am OK".

All of these beliefs are a trap that keep us in hell, they keep us from listening to music, or smiling, or even from loving again. We believe that somehow our living has something to do with honoring or dishonoring the person that died. I love doing a visualization exercise with my patients when this belief comes up. I ask them to close their eyes and "pull up" in their mind, the person who has died. (It usually takes a 1/2 of a second). I ask them to describe what they see, what their loved one is wearing, where are they located. Then I ask them to tell their deceased loved one how it has been for them, here after their death. Usually, what is heard back is some type of acknowledgment of the pain and sadness of separation. Then I ask them to pose a question to their loved one: " What do I do now that you have died?" In all of my years of counseling, with the thousands of people who I have had the honor of working with, have I ever heard the response be, "You know, I want you to live a painful and miserable life full of suffering and devoid of joy. And if you do not, that would be dishonoring me". If I pose this response to my patients, they usually burst out laughing and follow it up with, "He/She would actually tell me to live a great life, be happy and have joy". Sometimes, the patient would follow it up with, "He/She would actually be really pissed off at me if I thought that living a crappy, miserable life is honoring them. The ultimate act of honoring him/her is by living well".

How about the belief," If I am happy, it means that I've moved on or that they don't matter anymore". Now there are 3 words that I will never say, to myself or to my patients and that is," We move on". These words connotes that we are leaving "them" "back there", and I don't know about you, but if I have to *leave* my kids, I'm not going. I like to say that I am moving, not forward, just living. We need to move to survive, to live, and that is what adaptation is all about, moving. Isn't this what we were seeking the moment that we were traumatized, we wanted relief? Our biggest fear was that we would lose the ability to feel happiness and joy again and now that we have it, we feel guilt, somehow committing a mortal sin to want relief. And what does feeling happy have anything to do with that person's importance? The minute that person came into our lives and the minute that they departed, they mattered. Their importance is sealed, so does somehow denying ourselves joy make them more special? Of course not and it is irrelevant.

Now what about the story that says "it's not fair, they didn't get more time so why should I?". We all have this imaginary, invisible hour glass that was given to us at birth, be it your belief in God, biology, fate or luck, to say that all are supposed to have the same or equal grains of sand is absurd and would quite frankly, in reality, be really scary. Look at what this belief does to me? It cuts off my life line, I want to throw myself down and have a big tantrum, adult style, that's what I call it. It's no different than when a toddler throws themselves down on the floor and screams or pouts. When I go to this place, I like to ask myself, "Who are you Laurie, God?". What is this concept of fairness or deserving? There is no such thing as fair. Usually our definition of fair is, "As long as I am getting what I want or expected, all is fair but the minute I don't, I feel cheated and it's unfair". And who is supposed to get more time? Less time? What is this concept of deserving? That somehow, because a person has died, they are wanting or if it is even possible to be "paid back" through our misery? As if they are looking down in us angry because we are here and they are not? It just doesn't make sense and the reason it doesn't is because it doesn't. It is coming from insane mind, mind out of truth. This is a human disposition, not a spiritual one. Just try it, close your eyes and call up the person who has died. You see them? OK, now tell them that you are going to be miserable and suffer here on earth out of solidarity and love for them because they did not get to be here longer. What do you hear as their response? This well-crafted story is based on the juxtaposition of two positions: freedom and obligation.

Love is free, it asks for nothing, not acknowledgment, fairness, payback, suffering, solidarity, praise, or understanding. It does not feel sad, guilty, scary, frustrating or intimidating. Love is patient, gentle and effortless, love feels calm, happy and confident. So is it love when we believe that we owe the people in our lives anything, whether they are alive or dead? Love is complete and kind and doesn't ask to prove itself or to be proven.

Love creates happiness, and happiness is a by-product that comes from living the life that we want to live, however long that is. I have traveled a million miles so that I could one day, feel that joy again, and that is honoring life, mine and theirs. When I summons Alec and Asher in my mind, I say, "Look at me Mumsie, look at how Mama is living". I always hear back, "I'm so proud of you Mama. You're such a good Mama". Tears always follow, however, different tears, they are tears of joy. I tell them that I love them, and I envision Alec coming close to my face and saying " It's OK Mom, it's OK". Just like he would do when he was here, in that other life. To me, that is love in the purest form.

IN CLOSING

I USED TO BELIEVE that my ability to journey out of hell was a miracle, but based solely on definition, I am not sure about that. A miracle is defined as," an amazing, beneficial event that goes against (or at least seems to) the laws of nature", but for me, it is on the contrary. Every experience that I have encountered has been met with a will to live, to preserve life and to love, and that is the pure essence of the laws of nature, to create, to grow, to recycle. All of my life experiences have prepared me to live in this exact moment in time, here, in truth, with you and that is not luck, it is the way of this auspicious universe, if we are paying attention.

It is me who is the recipient of great fortune, for I am sitting under a shade fruit tree because someone before me planted the tree. It is me who relishes in the fruits of their plantings. I am so grateful for all that has been passed on and entrusted to me and I generously give it all away. I claim nor seek any recognition, praise or credit for the lessons that I impart, for we all are teachers and students of the priceless bounty that lives in this vast ocean of life.

And I did not travel alone in my quest for this holy grail, I am with many. Those who I claim as my most trusted confidants to the invisible stranger who has supported me by showing up for work so I could have electricity to power this computer that I impart my words to you on. I am blessed to have all, the ones who love me and the ones who are less than favorable, all are my teachers that hold my mirrors.

It is ironic that I complete this book that was born in me long ago on Mother's Day. I may not know you and you may not know me, but I am humbled that you have chosen to spend your time, those precious invisible grains of sand, by reading my book.

It is me who is the fortunate and humbled recipient of your attention. However, this book found its way to you, be it in your quest for relief or answers, maybe as a gift, or simply stumbled upon in surfing the web, I shamelessly share all of me with you. I invite you to seek out your true wisdom which lies with awareness and action in finding the truth, your truth as I have done for myself.

With love and life,
Laurie Beth

WWLS
(WHAT WOULD LAURIE SAY?)

WE LIVE INSIDE OF each other, so here are a few Laurie Be-thisms that I impart to you if you so choose to have me take up some of your mental real estate....

Life is unpredictable and control is an illusion.

I will never, ever leave my children. If I can't go there, then I will bring them here.

Why isn't happiness a good enough reason to do something?

Never allow anyone or anything to be so powerful as to make you feel happy or unhappy.

We are not our stories, but our stories can become us.

Remember, focus on process, not outcome. Outcome is none of our business.

Never, ever, believe that you have to prove yourself to anyone, not even yourself.

Adaptation to the death of my kids is kinder and gentler than forcing myself into acceptance.

Pain may be involuntary but suffering is voluntary.

Treat yourself as if you didn't have a separate set of rules for yourself.

Mind your own business.

If suffering would bring back the ones we love, then I would suffer for a lifetime, but it won't, so I choose to be happy.

CPSIA information can be obtained
at www.ICGtesting.com
Printed in the USA
LVOW10s1450030218
565195LV00006B/82/P